You and
Your Camera

Only a camera could capture the excitement and beauty of rushing water.

Lou Jacobs, Jr.

YOU
AND YOUR
CAMERA

ILLUSTRATED WITH PHOTOGRAPHS

Lothrop, Lee & Shepard Company

New York

ACKNOWLEDGMENTS

Photographs have been provided through the courtesy of the following:

Figures 1, 6, 10, 11, 12, 23, 25, 28, 30, 31, 32, 33, 46, 53, 54, 55, 56, 57,
    58, 60, 61, 62, 63, 64, 65, 66, 67, 68, 69, 70, 71, 81, 82, 84, 85, 86,
    87, 90, 92, 93—Eastman Kodak Company
Figure 2—Mathew Brady Collection, Library of Congress
Figure 3—Library of Congress
Figure 4—L. A. County Museum
Figure 5—National Aeronautics and Space Administration
Figure 7—Polaroid
Figure 13—Father Bernard Hubbard Photo
Figures 26, 27—Konica
Figure 35—Hawaii Visitors Bureau Photo
Figure 40—Barbara Jacobs Photo
Figure 59—Bob Noble Photo
Figure 76—Harvey Hill Photo

All other photographs were taken by the author

Contents

You and
Your Camera

Introduction

Photography is one of the most popular hobbies in the world. This is so because everyone with a camera enjoys taking pictures and later looking at slides and prints of people he knows, places he has been, and things he has done. A painter or a photographer must learn to see very sharply in order to make appealing pictures. But a painter works by hand and has one copy of his picture, while a photographer works with a mechanical camera and may have many copies of his pictures. A painter make take weeks to create his scene or portrait, but a photographer can snap many images in a short time. The super-speed of photography can lead to carelessness, but both photographs and paintings made by sensitive people can be fine, artistic pictures.

Here is a short list of things you can do with your camera:

1. You can shoot slides or movies and have prints made of anything you can see, from distant mountains to the face of a friend.

2. Your pictures can make people laugh, feel sad, get angry, or help them see something new.

3. Your photograph in color or black and white can be saved in an album, or hung on the wall to be enjoyed every day.

4. Pictures help make new friends and please old ones.

Photographs are everywhere: in newspapers, magazines and books, on television, and in movie theaters. A knowledge of photography helps you to understand and appreciate the photographs you see everywhere around you.

Photography began in 1826, when a Frenchman named

Figure 1—This is flash photography in the early years of the century, which was inconvenient and could be hazardous as well.

Figure 2—Photography from the past shows us people, places, and things that we could not see otherwise. In this photograph, taken in August 1862 by T. H. O. Sullivan, fugitive blacks forge the Rappahanock River in Virginia.

Joseph Niepce made the first permanent photograph. His exposures sometimes took eight hours! Another Frenchman, named Louis Daguerre, caused a sensation in 1839 with his pictures on metal plates called daguerrotypes. People had to sit still for only a minute in order to be photographed. Hundreds

11

Figure 3—Here is a daguerrotype of Abraham Lincoln with his son Tad.

of men and women helped to pioneer photography. We can see their pictures of American cities when muddy streets were filled with horses and wagons. We have Mathew Brady's photographs of Civil War battlefields and famous people who died long ago. Today, because of photography, we have watched a man land on the moon; we have seen the development of a baby inside its mother; and we witness baseball and football games as they happen.

The first chapter of this book is for beginners who use simple cameras that do not have to be adjusted for exposure time or focus. The Instamatic-type camera, box cameras, and brownies are simple cameras. The rest of the book is for all camera fans who want to be sure of the results when they photograph a beautiful sunset or people at a party.

Simple cameras can cost as little as 5 dollars, while better cameras may cost 100 dollars or more. However, you don't need an expensive camera at the beginning. Slowly, as you understand more about picture-taking, you can hope for (and deserve!) a better camera with adjustments that allow you to

Figure 4—Famous flyer Amelia Earhart with her favorite car and airplane.

shoot a wider variety of pictures. Perhaps someone in your family has an adjustable camera you can borrow when you are ready. As your skill develops and your pictures improve, I hope you will have a good camera of your own.

This book should help you use photographic equipment intelligently. I hope you will read it and come back to read parts again. When older members of your family admire your pictures, you can lend them the book. They may also want to learn the things you discovered in these pages.

Figure 5—Apollo 11 astronaut Edwin E. Aldrin, Jr., stands by the American flag just planted on the moon. The photographer was Neil A. Armstrong, the first man to set foot on the moon.

15

1 | For Beginners

Most young people shoot pictures of friends and family and places they visit. If you have a camera, do you get good pictures with it? Do you get enough of them? Your answer may depend on what you consider "good." A snapshot that is taken carefully may be very good, but a snapshot taken carelessly may show mistakes that are your fault. Until you know what you are doing with your camera, you waste time and money. It is not difficult to learn how you and your camera can work together for *good* pictures.

INSIDE YOUR CAMERA

Figure 6 shows the parts of a simple camera. Figure 14 (on page 30) shows how a picture is taken. In quick review, the lens is like an eye that "sees" the scene. You look through the finder window. When you push the shutter button, the shutter

16

winding knob

flash cube

shutter button

finder window

INSTAMATIC 44
CAMERA
MADE IN U.S.A.
Kodak

lens

Figure 6—A simple camera with parts identified.

opens and closes quickly. An image passes through the lens and is picked up on the film. You turn the winding knob to bring new film behind the lens and cock the shutter. Now you are set to take another picture.

A simple camera without adjustments has a lens that takes pictures best in bright light. It will also take pictures in bright shade or on a bright cloudy day. When there is not enough light outdoors or indoors, you use a flashcube or flashbulb. A cube plugs into the top of the camera. As you wind the film, the flashcube turns, ready for the next shot.

CAMERAS FOR BEGINNERS

The most popular cameras are simple and easy to use. Most of them take Instamatic-type film (size 126 cartridge) or 127 roll

17

Figure 7—This is the inexpensive Polaroid Colorpack II camera. On top is the finder, the lens is in the center, and the shutter button is above and at the left of the lens. Beside the lens is the electric-eye window, next to which is a place to plug in flashcubes.

film. You get twelve pictures on each roll. A few simple cameras have a setting you can adjust for bright sun, flash, or shade. This setting regulates the amount of light that reaches the film and could help you get better pictures. Many simple cameras are designed to prevent double exposures, which means you cannot shoot one picture on top of another. Cameras for beginners are made by Kodak, GAF, Argus, Revere, Wards, and several other companies.

Polaroid Land cameras are also popular for beginners. You do have to focus a Polaroid, which means you set the lens for the distance in feet between the camera and the subject. The

Polaroid regulates its own exposure, and your prints are ready in a minute or less.

If you don't have a camera, try to save between 10 and 25 dollars to buy one, or ask someone to give it to you for Christmas or your birthday. It is good to start with a camera of your own, even an inexpensive one. You can look forward to using or having a better camera when you are ready. Christmas and your birthday come every year! Talk to someone in your family about what camera to buy, and ask the man in the camera shop to help you choose.

ABOUT FILMS

Black and white films are usually faster than color films. This means you can take pictures in black and white with less light than you need for color. Black and white films and prints cost less than color films and prints. Since you are likely to waste some pictures in the beginning, try black and white film for your first few rolls. You can learn as much without shooting color, and you save money. The most popular black and white film is Verichrome Pan.

There are two types of color film. From color-*negative* film (such as Kodacolor or GAF Color Print Film) you get negatives and color prints. You can have slides made from the negatives later if you wish. Most beginners use color-negative film because they prefer to have prints rather than slides.

When you shoot color-*positive* film, you get slides, also called transparencies. You hold a slide up to the light to see the picture, or put it into a projector and see it on a screen. The most popular slide films are Kodachrome II, Ektachrome, Anscochrome, and Agfachrome.

Many companies develop color film and make prints at special prices. Some send you a new roll of film with each order. You might try one of these deals, but sometimes the film you get back is not as good as the film you buy at the camera shop.

ABOUT LIGHT

Bright sunlight—If you have heard someone say "Shoot with the sun behind you," it is *not* advice to follow all the time. Good pictures are often taken when the sun shines from one side of your subject or the other. Around noon, when the sun is high overhead, the light is not as good for pictures as when the sun

Figure 8—This is a pleasant snapshot in either black and white or color. The light comes from one side, you can see what the people are doing clearly, and there is no wasted space around the edges.

Figure 9—A simple camera could take this kind of picture. It is easy to see the story of children fishing, and none of them were moving too fast as the picture was snapped.

slants at an angle in the morning or afternoon. This is because the shadows from diagonal sunlight are more interesting than shadows from the noonday sun.

You can also shoot pictures when the sun is shining almost into your lens. Shade the lens with one hand, or you will get a fuzzy effect on your prints or slides.

21

Hazy sunlight and cloudy days—Some simple cameras take pictures very well when the sunlight is hazy or the sky is cloudy. Other simple cameras do not have large-enough lenses, and pictures in hazy sun or on a cloudy day will be too dark. If your camera seems to do well under these conditions, the colors you get are usually very pretty. Take pictures whether there is sun or not, for in this way you will learn to judge the light.

Sometimes a short time exposure will do well when it is dark or the light is dim. If your camera has a time-exposure setting, hold the camera firmly on a table indoors or on a rock outdoors. The camera must not move even a tiny bit during a time exposure.

ABOUT FLASHCUBES AND FLASHBULBS

When there is not enough light and you cannot take a time exposure because your subject is moving, you need a flashcube or flashbulb. Use flash in the shade, after sunset, indoors, or after dark anywhere. Flashcubes and flashbulbs both work the same way, and simple cameras use one or the other. Since you cannot make the light from a flashcube or flashbulb stronger or weaker, remember these three things:

1. If what you are shooting is more than 10 feet away, your flash may be too weak for good pictures.

2. If you shoot something as close as three or four feet, your flash may be too bright, but good prints can often be made anyway.

3. If you stand between four and nine feet from a subject, flash light will usually be good.

22

Figure 10—One flashcube or flashbulb on the camera was used for this nice picture of a cat by Philip Lee, aged sixteen. His picture, which won a prize in the *Scholastic*/Kodak Awards contest, was enlarged. Some of the negative was not printed because it did not help the picture.

23

Figure 11—The lens of a simple camera does not always take sharp pictures, but this snapshot by John Monohan, aged thirteen, another prize winner, tells a story. John took the picture in color.

HINTS FOR TAKING BETTER PICTURES

1. *Hold your camera steady.* Take a breath and *squeeze* the shutter button. Don't snap quickly or you will jerk the camera, and the picture will not be sharp. More pictures are not sharp because of camera movement than because of any other mistake.

2. *Stand close enough to your subject.* Too many snapshots are taken with someone "way out there" so he is very small in the print or slide. Move close enough to get a large image of the person or thing that is important. Leave out unimportant things and fill the space.

3. *Try for good expressions.* Some people look straight at the camera and look kind of frozen. Young people often make funny faces. Ask for a smile if you want a good expression. Anything you can say to make people feel at ease will help your pictures.

4. *Watch the background.* If there are poles, wires, or strange shapes in the background, move the camera or ask the person to move so the background is plainer. Look carefully at the scene and leave out shapes or objects that are in the way beside or behind the subject.

5. *Shoot when the action slows down.* Simple cameras are not fast enough to shoot action sharply when people or things are moving rapidly. For instance, if you photograph someone batting a ball, wait until he or she swings and stops for a second. Then shoot. You will get sharper pictures.

6. *Keep your pictures as simple as possible.* The best pictures are usually fairly simple in the way things are arranged. They have one main shape (such as a person or thing) and several smaller shapes, and the background is simple as well.

7. *Be sure there is enough light.* If there is so little light that when you squint you see very little detail in a subject, use flash. Dark prints and slides indicate that the film was not fast enough for the amount of light available.

8. *Keep your camera clean.* Keep your fingers off the lens and finder. Keep water and dirt away from your camera. Carry it

25

Figure 12—This is a good example of keeping a picture simple. The sky makes a good background, and the camera was held very steady by Bruce Rapoport, aged seventeen, who won a *Scholastic*/Kodak Award.

in a small case to keep it clean. Don't scratch a flashcube or flashbulb, or it may be unsafe to use.

9. *Load and unload your camera in the shade.* Strong light may get inside your film cartridge or roll. This light can create streaks that spoil your prints or slides.

SAVING YOUR PICTURES

The prints you like best should be put in an album. There are large and small albums at many prices. Choose one and mount your good prints in it. Put a date on the back of each print, and

Figure 13—This nice Eskimo family was photographed by Father Bernard Hubbard, who explored Alaska many years ago. His pictures are well preserved, and show us how people looked fifty years or more in the past.

under each print on the album page. Keeping your pictures orderly makes them more fun to look at later. You will remember that beautiful lake where you caught the fish, and you can easily find a picture of the fish to show a friend.

Keep your negatives in separate envelopes and date the envelopes. Keep negatives in a box. When you want to find one to have a print made, you will know where it is.

Store slides in the boxes in which they come, and date the boxes. You may also store slides in the trays or boxes used in a projector. If you keep your slides in the same place that your family does, mark yours to find them easily.

If you have a picture you like especially well, ask your mother or dad to have an enlargement made. Have the enlargement mounted on heavy cardboard. You will be proud to see it on your wall.

LEARNING MORE ABOUT PHOTOGRAPHY

Before you go on to the following chapters in this book, you should be sure you know and understand the things you read in this chapter. You might ask yourself these questions: Am I proud of my pictures? Do I know how to correct mistakes I make? Do I know the parts of my camera and understand how they work? Can I take care of my camera? Do I care enough for my prints or slides to save them in an album or store them away safely?

It is easy to learn to use a simple camera carefully, and better pictures are your reward. Don't be a camera fan who just points the camera, presses the shutter button, and hopes for the best. You will be disappointed.

As your pictures improve, there are more things to know

about using a camera when you are ready. When you have a better camera with adjustments for exposure and focus, you can shoot fast action, closeups, or in dim light without flash. Photography can be as creative as painting a picture or playing the piano. All of these things take effort. You and your camera are a team that make the effort worthwhile.

2 | How a Camera Works

A camera is a light-tight box with a lens on one side and film inside the box opposite the lens. The lens "sees" the image you want to photograph. When you press a button, a shutter inside the camera opens and closes very rapidly. The image passes through the lens and is recorded on the film, which is sensitive to light. You advance the film to be ready for the next picture. The parts of a camera are illustrated in Figure 14.

Figure 14—Parts of a camera.

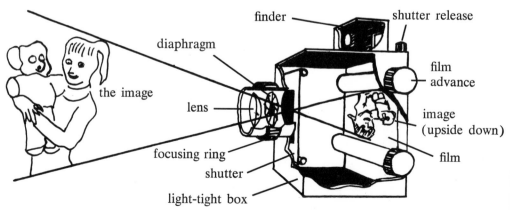

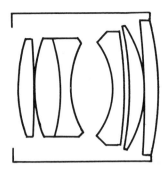

Figure 15—Inside a 55 mm. f/2 lens. This cutaway view of six pieces, or elements, of glass shows how they are arranged inside the lens.

There are many types of cameras, and those you will be most interested in are described in Chapters 1 and 3. A *simple camera* that does not focus and cannot be adjusted for exposure is best for beginners. A *single-lens reflex* camera is the most popular type of 35 mm. camera and most fun to use. A *rangefinder* camera is also a 35 mm. camera, and some models are inexpensive, which makes them useful for new photography fans.

PARTS OF A 35 MM. CAMERA
AND HOW THEY WORK

The lens—A lens consists of several pieces of special glass, ground to precise shapes and mounted in a cylinder called the barrel. A lens collects rays of light reflected from a scene and "draws" or projects them as an image on film. There are as many ways to shape and arrange the glass (called lens elements) in a lens as there are to arrange the furniture in your living room. Figure 15 shows the cutaway side view of a typical 55 mm. lens. Other lenses include more or fewer elements put together in many ways according to the angle of view and speed of the lens.

31

Lens openings—Inside a lens is a circle of thin, overlapping pieces of metal called a diaphragm. When you turn a ring on the outside of the lens, this circle opens and closes. The size of the diaphragm hole regulates the amount of light that passes through to the film. This diaphragm hole is called the aperture, or the lens stop, or the f/stop. The diaphragm is closed to a small aperture or opening for a bright scene and a larger aperture for a dimly lit scene.

The widest aperture of a simple camera is the only one you use because the lens, usually molded plastic, has no diaphragm. All 35 mm. cameras have adjustable f/stops that allow you to make small changes in exposure so important for good color slides or prints.

Figure 16 is a diagram of the standard f/stops or lens open-

Figure 16— Diagram of f/stop lens openings.

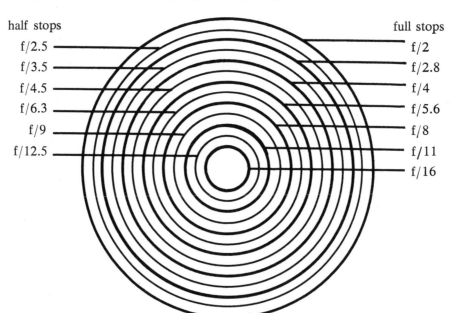

half stops	full stops
f/2.5	f/2
f/3.5	f/2.8
f/4.5	f/4
f/6.3	f/5.6
f/9	f/8
f/12.5	f/11
	f/16

ings you need to memorize. Though lenses vary in length and diameter, each is made so that any f/stop on one lens gives the same exposure as the same f/stop on another. As f/stop numbers get larger, each allows *half* the amount of light to enter the camera as the one before. As the numbers become smaller, each admits *twice* the amount of light as the one before. Half stops are used as a convenience to describe exposure settings between full f/stop numbers.

Where is a lens the sharpest?—No camera lens is sharpest at its widest opening because of the way glass is ground and elements must be arranged. When the diaphragm is stopped down about two stops, maximum sharpness begins. The average lens is sharpest in the middle range. For instance, an f/2 lens is usually sharpest between f/5.6 and f/11. However, the difference in sharpness between this middle range and f/16 is hard to see.

Depth of field—This is a very important term in photography that describes how much of a scene is in focus from the front to the back, at a given f/stop and a given distance from the camera. Figure 17 charts the depth of field range of a 55 mm. lens focused at 10 feet. Notice that sharpness increases away from the camera to a greater extent than it does closer to the camera.

In the instruction books that come with most 35 mm. cameras there are usually charts or tables that show exact depth of the field for various lenses. After you study these tables for the lens(es) you have, you will know how much of a scene will be sharp if you set your focus at 10 feet, for instance, and must snap a picture quickly without focusing again. Here are some tips about depth of field:

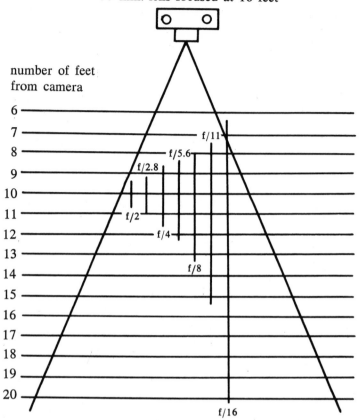

Figure 17—How depth of field works. Straight lines show the depth of the area in focus at different apertures.

1. Short-focal-length lenses (focal length is explained in the next section), such as 28 mm. or 35 mm., offer greater depth of field at a given f/stop and distance than longer-focal-length lenses. This is a law of optics, or the science of lenses.

2. The closer you focus to an object or a face, the less depth of field you have. In Figure 18 the camera was about 3 feet from the girl's face, which is sharp, but her ear and the back of her

Figure 18—The area in focus, or depth of field, is not very large when you are close for a portrait like this. The camera was about 3 feet from the girl's face, and the back of her hair is slightly out of focus.

35

neck are slightly out of focus. This is not important, but remember, when you shoot a portrait, focus on the eyes. When your camera is only a foot or two from a subject, your depth of field may be only a few inches.

3. The smaller your aperture, the more depth of field you get. Figure 19 is an example of this statement. The camera was on a tripod, and the f/stop was f/22. The lens was focused at about the third fencepost back, and the small aperture gave me sharp focus from the front fencepost to the trees behind this old barn in Northern California. If I had shot at f/8 instead, either the front fenceposts or the old barn would have been out of focus.

Figure 19—A smaller aperture increased the depth of field in this picture.

4. On the lens barrel of most lenses for 35 mm. cameras, opposite the diaphragm opening ring, are a series of f/stop numbers, the same on both sides of the center marker. This is the depth-of-field scale, and it shows you approximately how many feet are in focus between the identical f/stop numbers.

5. Looking through the lens of a single-lens-reflex camera, you can check depth of field approximately by closing the aperture to the f/stop you need.

What is lens focal length?—This term describes the distance from the lens to the film, and is usually measured in millimeters (mm.). Knowing the focal length of a lens is important, because it tells you if the lens "sees" a wider or narrower area than the normal lens that comes with the camera. Lenses are made in dozens of focal lengths. Here is a list:

1. Wide-angle: 21 mm., 28 mm., and 35 mm.

2. Normal: 50 mm., 52 mm., and 55 mm.

3. Long: 85 mm., 105 mm., and 135 mm.

4. Telephoto: Any length longer than 135 mm.

Of course, you can do very well with just the normal lens that comes with your camera. However, a wide-angle or a long lens increases your chances for shooting when you cannot move closer to a subject or away from it. As a sample of how three popular focal-length lenses show a scene, look at Figures 20, 21, and 22. Figure 20 was shot with a 35 mm. lens, Figure 21 was shot with a 55 mm. lens and Figure 22 is the same scene from the same spot with a 135 mm. lens. These pictures also show how you can vary a composition from a single point of view by changing lenses.

When you or someone in your family is ready for additional

Figure 20—A 35 mm. wide-angle lens made a wide image on the film.

Figure 21—The normal 55 mm. lens showed a smaller area, but the buildings are larger.

Figure 22—From the same spot a 135 mm. lens enlarged the image as a telescope does.

lenses, check the zoom lenses available as well. A zoom lens changes focal length as you turn a ring on the outside of the barrel. A zoom lens is longer and heavier than a lens of a single focal length, but one zoom lens can take the place of many individual lenses.

How a shutter works—There are two types of camera shutters. The *leaf* type opens its fanlike blades and closes them again at the end of an exposure. The *focal-plane* shutter (used on most 35 mm. cameras) is like a window shade that flips across, or up and down, in front of the film. You adjust the speeds on a shutter by turning a dial marked in fractions of a second. Each fraction allows half (for instance from 1/60th to 1/125th of a second) or twice (1/60th to 1/30th of a second) the exposure of the last one.

Tiny springs inside the camera make a shutter work at dif-

39

Figure 23—A fast shutter speed of 1/500th of a second froze the swimmer's action in this fine shot by Michael Mulvena, aged sixteen (*Scholastic*/Kodak Award winner). You can feel the swimmer trying hard and can almost hear the water splash.

ferent speeds. These springs will work longer and better if you put a camera away with the shutter not cocked.

To avoid fuzzy pictures and stop action properly when you shoot outdoors, shoot at 1/125th of a second or faster. If the highest shutter speed on your camera is 1/500th of a second, it's fast enough to photograph anything from a football runner to a friend diving. Slow shutter speeds are used when the light is dim and you prefer not to use flash because you like the existing light.

Built-in exposure meters—The meter in a 35 mm. camera sees through the lens of a single-lens reflex, or beside the lens of a rangefinder camera. A small cell inside the meter senses the amount of light and electrically operates a needle you see at the edge of the finder. By adjusting the shutter speed or the f/stop, you center the needle and you are set for correct exposure. In a few 35 mm. cameras, such as those made by Konica, the meter sets the f/stop automatically, which is both fast and convenient.

It is very important that you read the instruction book that comes with your 35 mm. camera. In it you will learn how that particular camera works, what lenses are made for it, and how to get better pictures. When you are familiar with lenses, the shutter, focusing, and other camera operations, you begin to think like a camera! You must depend on the camera and its meter to give you good slides or prints, but you can handle this wonderful instrument as easily as a carpenter cuts wood with an electric saw.

Figure 24—If your camera has a built-in exposure meter, it is easy to get the proper exposure for a scene like this one, which was taken in Arizona. You must be careful not to tilt the camera toward the sky too much or the picture will be underexposed.

3 | The Tools of Photography

CAMERAS

In the average camera shop there are many types and brands of cameras. What should you buy? How can you be sure to get your money's worth? What other equipment do you really need? Let us consider these questions, one by one.

Cameras costing between 10 and 25 dollars usually have few adjustments for lens openings, shutter speeds, or focus. They are quite suitable for beginners, and easier to use than the old "box cameras" or "brownies" your mother and dad started with. In the price range from 25 to 150 dollars there is great variety. You can focus most of these cameras, and adjust the lens openings and shutter speeds for different kinds of light. The more expensive cameras, and I'm talking here about 35 mm. cameras, have removable lenses. When you change from one

42

lens to another, you see a view that is wider or narrower than the lens that comes with the camera. More expensive cameras put you in the big leagues with skilled and serious photographers.

There is such a large selection of simple and 35 mm. cameras that shopping for one can be confusing. I hope you will have a better idea of what to look for when you read on. Many cameras are made in Japan, while others are made in Germany and the United States. Today the country in which photographic equipment is made is *no* indication of its quality. Fine 35 mm. cameras come from all three countries as well as from Switzerland.

Simple cameras—A simple, inexpensive camera is usually a hard plastic box with a lens, a finder, and a place to plug in a flashcube or a flash reflector. The most popular simple cameras are the Instamatic type, made by several companies. (Instamatic is a Kodak trademark; this type of camera uses a drop-in film cartridge. Eastman Kodak makes a series of Instamatic cameras, and some of the more expensive ones are not "simple" cameras at all.) With simple cameras you need rather bright light or flash to shoot. You cannot focus the lens or change the exposure on most. Pictures are not as sharp as those taken by more expensive cameras, but they are often quite satisfactory.

35 mm. cameras—Open a recent copy of *Popular Photography* or *Modern Photography,* or glance at the shelves in a camera shop, and you will realize how many 35 mm. cameras are on sale today. A majority of them are the single-lens-reflex type (SLR). This means that when you look through the finder you see the same image through the lens that you snap on the film.

Figure 25—The latest Kodak Instamatic cameras use a new kind of flashcube called a Magicube, which can be fired without battery power. They range in price from 21 dollars for the X-15 (bottom left) to 31 dollars for the X-25 (bottom right) and 48 dollars for the X-35 (top right).

A few 35 mm. cameras use a rangefinder to focus the lens, which means the finder is separate from the lens. Among the brand names you will see are Nikon, Topcon, Pentax, Mamiya, Canon, Ricoh, Yashica, Konica, Leica, Minolta, Miranda, Petri, Exakta, Practica, and Kodak. From this wide selection, how do you choose?

First you need to know the similarities and differences between brands and models. Read the ads, send for brochures, and approach a dealer's counter armed with basic information.

Handle the cameras that appeal to you, and ask plenty of questions. How does the camera feel? Is it too heavy? Can you see through the finder comfortably, especially if you wear glasses? How much do additional lenses cost? Does the camera have features you don't actually need that help boost the price?

Figure 26—A 35 mm. single-lens reflex camera. From the left on top are the film advance lever, the shutter button, the film speed dial, and the rewind knob at right. In front is the lens. The small button to the left of the lens releases the lens to be removed. The first row of numbers on top of the lens is the footage scale for focusing. The second row of numbers is the depth-of-the-field scale, and the third row indicates the f-stop marks.

Figure 27—A 35 mm. rangefinder camera. With the back open you can see where the film cartridge goes at left.

46

What to spend—If you know you can spend no more than a certain amount for a 35 mm. camera, this will help limit your choice. A camera with an exposure meter built into it costs more than one without a meter. However, the convenience of a built-in meter is worth having if you can afford it. If you cannot remove the lens from a 35 mm. rangefinder camera, it will cost less than SLR cameras with removable, or interchangable, lenses. Being able to change lenses is important when photography becomes a more serious hobby. A 35 mm. camera with lenses that screw in may cost less than one with bayonet-mount lenses. Both systems work very well. Bayonet-mount lenses are faster to change, but there are far more screw-mount lenses on the market at reasonable prices.

You do not need a self-timer on your first 35 mm. camera, nor do you need a shutter speed as fast as 1/1000th of a second. Models without these features save you money. Do not be hypnotized by cameras with widely advertised brand names. They are usually excellent, but less well-known equipment may serve you as well and cost less.

Buying on trial—Arrange to buy your 35 mm. camera on a one-week or ten-day trial basis. You can return it for another model if you are not satisfied. Test the new camera carefully so a dealer can resell it if you take it back. Shoot one or two rolls of film in various kinds of light at many lens openings and shutter speeds. Decide whether the slides or prints look well-exposed. Your confidence in a camera at this early stage will pay off in better pictures.

You cannot be certain about the durability of any camera. When you make a choice, ask at the camera shop about the repair record of that model. All cameras eventually have problems in the shutter or in the film-advance mechanism. You are protected for at least one year by a guarantee. Some cameras work well for years without repairs, while others need attention every year or two. This cannot be predicted, even by brand name.

Buying a used camera—As the saying goes, it's "cool" to buy a used 35 mm. camera from a reliable dealer. The guarantee is usually about ninety days. A used camera should cost twenty-five percent to fifty percent less than a new one, and could be well worth it if it is in good condition.

Buying a used camera from an individual can be risky because you get no guarantee. Make a down payment and sign a note promising to pay the rest of the money after you have tested the camera. Some faults are hard to discover unless you take pictures. If the price is very reasonable, you might be able to afford small repairs and still get a good deal. A used camera might be dirty inside, and cleaning a 35 mm. camera can cost between 20 and 35 dollars.

Half-frame 35 mm. cameras—These compact models take two pictures in the same area of film that yields one 35 mm. picture, or use special miniature film. Half-frame cameras are handy for travel because they are small, but their negatives or slides do not enlarge as well as a full 35 mm. frame (the word used for one picture on a roll). Brand names include Minox, Rollei 16, Mamiya 16, Petri, and Tessina.

2¼ x 2¼ cameras—Unless you need a larger negative or slide (120 size) for a good reason, you don't need a 2¼ x 2¼ camera. They are heavier and bulkier than 35 mm. cameras, and are needed more often by professionals, whose pictures may be enlarged to billboard size. Brand names of these larger cameras include Rolleiflex, Hassleblad, Bronica, Yashica, Mamiya, and Minolta.

Polaroid Land cameras—There are many models with added automatic features as they increase in price. Polaroid film is pulled from the back of the camera, and prints develop in ten seconds (black and white) or one minute (color). A Polaroid may help you to learn photography because you can see and correct your mistakes immediately. Pictures that can be developed in a minute are also useful for making friends in strange places or to please visiting relatives. A Polaroid camera sets its own exposure by using an electric eye. Prints cost a little more than those you get from conventional film.

STILL CAMERA LENSES

After you have learned to use a 35 mm. camera and one lens, more lenses add to the pleasure of photography. Hundreds of lenses are made for 35 mm. cameras. Some are of the same brand name as your camera, and some are made by other companies, such as Vivitar, Soligor, Tamron, Komura, Spiratone, or Accura. They have a very wide range of prices. A 35 mm. wide-angle lens, for instance, may cost between 40 and 125 dollars. Since lenses are designed by computers today, most are reasonably sharp. Only testing will tell whether a 50 dollar lens will serve you as well as a 100 dollar lens.

To test a lens, place your camera on a tripod and take some pictures. Have them enlarged or project the slides on a screen. Decide whether the images are sharp enough to suit you and the color looks right. Don't be tempted to buy a lens because

49

it has a very large aperture. An f/2 lens will do as well for you as an f/1.5, and save you many dollars. If your camera has a normal lens such as the 50 mm., the 52 mm., or the 55 mm., a good choice of additional lenses might be a 35 mm. and a 105 mm, or 135 mm. telephoto.

Lenses for SLR cameras are made in two types: automatic and pre-set. An automatic lens is wide open as you focus. Its aperture closes itself when you shoot a picture and opens itself again afterwards. You have to open and close a pre-set lens by hand. Automatic lenses cost more, but they are more convenient to use. An automatic lens assures consistent exposures since you can't forget to close the aperture before you shoot. Automatic lenses are certainly worth their extra cost.

Figure 28—A 35 mm. single-lens reflex camera (without a lens on the body) and the selection of lenses available for it. In front is the normal 45 mm. lens and behind the camera is a 200 mm. telephoto.

Figure 29—Interesting effects are possible with a slow shutter speed. I sat with this young man in a giant teacup at Disneyland. As it twirled around, I exposed at 1/30th of a second with my 35 mm. camera. The blur in the background adds to the feeling of movement.

CHOOSING COLOR FILMS

Some photographic films are faster than others, which means they are more sensitive to light. A fast film allows you to shoot in places where the light is weak. In bright sunlight, however, you may not want all the speed of a fast film, because you cannot stop your lens down (or close the aperture) far enough.

Films are rated by ASA (ASA stands for American Standards Association, which invented the film ratings) numbers or by EI (Exposure Index) numbers. Slow film such as Kodachrome

51

II is rated at ASA 25. A medium-speed film such as Ekta-chrome-X is ASA 64, and Ektacolor-X is ASA 80. A fast color film is High Speed Ektachrome (ASA 160). Anscochrome is made in four ASA speeds: 64, 100, 200, and 500. These are the numbers you use to set the exposure meter dial on your camera (or on a separate meter) according to the film you choose.

Except for Ektacolor-X, all the films mentioned above are *transparency* films. This means you get a box of slides when they are developed. Color prints or black and white prints can be made from the slides when a negative is made first.

If you prefer to get color prints first, choose a negative color film such as Kodacolor-X. Color slides or black and white prints can also be made from color negatives. Kodacolor and similar negative films are best for beginners, while more experienced camera fans may prefer to shoot color slides and project them.

You should try all of these films so you can compare them. When you find which one or two you like best, stick with it. When you are familiar with a film, it gives you confidence to get better pictures.

You might also try an indoor, or tungsten, type of color film. Two names are High Speed Ektachrome Type B and Koda-chrome II Type A. The former is used with flood bulbs marked 3200°K, and the latter with regular photoflood bulbs. If you use an indoor film and want to shoot pictures outdoors, you need an 85B filter with Ektachrome and an 85A filter with Koda-chrome.

Shooting pictures in color is a joy, whether you end up with slides or prints. It is fun to try different films to see what they will do for you.

Figure 30—Darrell Converse, aged twelve, used a close-up lens on his 35 mm. camera to shoot this portrait of his cat. The picture was a color award winner in the *Scholastic*/Kodak competition.

CHOOSING BLACK AND WHITE FILMS

The speed of black and white films is also slow, medium, and fast. A slow film, such as Panatomic-X (ASA 40), is called fine-grained. This means that big enlargements will not show the tiny grain pattern of the chemicals that make the film sensitive to light. However, if you use a slow film, you must shoot in fairly bright light or use flash.

A medium-speed film, such as Plus-X (ASA 125) or Verichrome Pan (ASA 125), may be best for beginners. Neither of them produce grain pattern that you will notice in prints.

53

Figure 31—Both color and black and white films are fast enough to take a picture of a racing car like this one by Larry Nutter, aged sixteen. (*Scholastic*/Kodak Award winner). Larry used a shutter speed of 1/250th of a second on his 35 mm. camera, and Tri-X film.

Use of a fast film such as Tri-X (ASA 400) makes pictures possible in dim light without flash. Big enlargements from a fast film will show some grain pattern, but usually not anything to worry about. Most of the pictures I took in this book were made with Tri-X, but you will probably be more comfortable with a slower film.

POLAROID LAND FILMS

Type 42 is rated at ASA 200, and Type 47 is ASA 3,000. The extreme speed of Type 47 often allows you to shoot without flash. Polacolor film is Type 108 (ASA 75) which makes color prints in one minute.

Temperature is important when you use any Polaroid Land film, especially color. When the air is cooler than 65°F, use the print warmer that comes with each camera to insure proper tones and color. Underdevelopment of Polaroid prints (when you pull them from the negative too soon) makes them dull and disappointing. However, a few seconds overdevelopment will not spoil your results.

54

EXPOSURE METERS

There are two types and many brands of exposure meters to use if your camera does not have one built in. The older type of meter uses a light-sensitive cell that measures light without battery power. The Weston meter is best known of this type (though Weston makes the newer type as well). The second type uses a cell powered by a tiny mercury battery, the kind used in cameras with built-in meters. The Luna-Pro is one of the best of these, but there are less-expensive models. You can buy a quite adequate exposure meter of either type for about 25 dollars, or less. More expensive models are able to measure much weaker light and are necessary for professional photographers.

You use an exposure meter in one of two ways. The first is by measuring light reflected from the subject. You point the meter at the scene and it averages the light and gives you a choice of f/stop and shutter-speed combinations. The second measures the incident light, or that which falls on the subject. You point the meter at the light source, such as the sun, and again the meter tells you a range of exposures. Both methods work well. In Chapter 5 a section about exposure explains how and when to use each type of light measurement.

If you have a camera with a built-in meter, do you need a separate exposure meter as well? Probably not—unless you do not trust the meter in your camera. When you are shooting against the light, an incident-light reading is more accurate than a reflected-light reading, and a camera meter measures only reflected light. However, you will discover how to do this by reading the booklet that comes with your camera. When you become more serious about photography as a hobby, you might have a separate meter as well to check exposures that are difficult for your camera meter.

Figure 32—This seascape on the coast of California illustrates the use of a long-focal-length lens and a camera on a tripod.

WHO NEEDS A TRIPOD?

If you want to be sure of picture sharpness, your camera must be held firmly when you shoot at 1/30th of a second or slower. The best tool for this is a tripod. Choose one that is comfortable to carry, but not too small. Miniature tripods that fold to about a foot long are easy to carry, but they are not usually very steady. Anyone needs a tripod to shoot long exposures of sunsets, or anywhere where the light is weak but useful.

GADGET BAGS AND CAMERA CASES

A snug fitting case may come with your 35 mm. camera, or it may be sold at additional cost. I suggest avoiding such camera cases because they get in the way and are unnecessary. The case hangs down when you are shooting, it adds weight around your neck, and it must be taken off to change film. Spend your money instead on a gadget bag just large enough to hold your camera(s), lenses, meter, film, and some lens-cleaning tissue. Your camera will be protected, and you will have everything you need in one place and within easy reach. Good gadget bags made of synthetic leather last a long time.

Figure 33—Mark Packo, aged seventeen, had his gadget bag handy when he photographed a football game in Ohio. He was able to change lenses on his camera easily, and this photo helped Mark win a scholarship in the *Scholastic*/Kodak competition.

USING FILTERS

A filter corrects the color of the light for color pictures or changes the tones in a black and white shot. Filters like the K2 (yellow), A (red), and G (orange) help to darken skies and make clouds stand out. A Polaroid filter is used to darken the sky and cut reflections as well. By revolving a Polaroid filter as you look through it, you can see the effect you will get.

The most useful filter for color transparency films is called a Skylight (1A). It helps to warm the color of shadows or a whole scene on a cloudy day. Ask your camera shop for a chart of filters and when to use them.

CHOOSING A SLIDE PROJECTOR

A slide projector costs from 50 to 250 dollars, and is most likely to be bought by your father or mother. The latest models include automatic focus (the image stays in focus even when heat might bend the slide a bit), brilliant quartz lamps, remote controls, and zoom lenses. Again, look at projectors at your camera shop or discount store (where cameras and film are also sold), and compare them. Most 35 mm. slide projectors do a good job, but automatic features, which add to the cost, offer easier operation.

TIPS ON OTHER EQUIPMENT

1. A lens hood or lens shade should be used at all times to reduce the light that enters the lens from the sides. A lens hood also helps to protect the lens from damage.

2. A lens extender is like a lens, but it screws into the camera, and your lens screws into the extender. The effect is to give the lens more magnifying power. An extender acts like another lens but costs less than a separate lens would.

3. Soft lens tissues are made to wipe delicate lenses. Use them instead of facial tissues or a handkerchief. Lens cleaning fluids are also available for use with lens tissue. Keep lenses free of fingerprints and dust, which spoil picture quality.

4. All kinds of dirt, water, and sand are the enemies of your camera and other equipment. However, if you think some kind of dirt may have gotten into the little springs and gears inside your camera, don't try to take it apart. That's a job for an expert camera repairman.

Buying a new camera can be exciting and fun. As you learn to use the camera, don't be afraid to try new films and new ways to take pictures. Don't buy camera equipment that you will be afraid to use. Don't be a camera fan who "falls in love" with beautiful, precise metal and glass, but fails to shoot photographs. You will meet people who talk about and display wonderful equipment, but you never see their pictures. It is better to own one camera, one lens, one gadget bag, and one tripod that you use with imagination than to have all sorts of equipment that just looks pretty on a shelf. After all, the photographer makes the pictures; the camera is just an instrument that does what *you* want it to do.

4 | Composition: The Way We See Things

The way subject matter is arranged in a photograph is called composition. The dictionary says composition is a combination of parts, or elements, to make a whole. A photographic composition may be interesting, exciting, dull, or somewhere in between. How do you know? What makes the difference?

The answers lie in the way your mind and eyes are trained to see and how skillful you are in capturing what you see on film. In any sort of picture there are elements of composition with which we work. These elements are lines, forms, textures, color, and the feeling of space. Let's find these elements in Figure 34, which I shot in Yellowstone National Park:

1. Lines—The thin trees and the edges of land and water

2. Forms—The land, the clouds and the mass of grass in the water

Figure 34—This picture has lines, forms, textures, space, and you can imagine the color.

3. Textures—The grass, the clouds and the trees

4. Color—Imagine the original greens, blues, and browns, plus the white clouds

5. Space—The feeling the eye gets as it travels from the foreground back into the picture, and high in the sky

Not everyone agrees on what a "good" composition is. Your own taste will develop as you study more about composition. Then you will understand better why certain pictures appeal to the judges of a contest or exhibition and you may not like them at all. Certain compositions are called conventional because they please many people. Other compositions are unusual because their arrangement is not conventional, but they are still attractive. An example of a conventional composition is the picture postcard, where everything seems to be in its place. When you have learned how to make good conventional compositions, you can try more unusual ways of taking pictures.

As an example of how composition may be analyzed, look at Figure 35, which came from the Hawaii Visitors Bureau. Some people might say the sailboat should have been slightly lower and to the right. Others may have included more beach in the foreground and less of the palm trees at the top. Before you decide whether these changes are right or wrong, ask yourself if they would have made the picture more interesting to look at.

Composition is a form of design which may be studied in junior high, high school, college, or from books. Each teacher and writer will have a point of view that will help develop your own taste. The best way to learn to compose a picture is to take lots of photographs and study them. Decide whether the horizon line is too high or too low in a landscape shot, whether a person is in the right spot in relation to the background, or whether the buildings in your snapshot have been photographed from the most pleasing angle. As you think about composition, you become more sensitive when looking through the finder of your camera.

I did not say there are "rules" for good composition because rules are rigid. You should be flexible in the way you see lines, forms, textures, colors, and space because your taste will change. Let's review some guidelines for composition.

Figure 35—Is the sailboat placed correctly? Would you prefer to see more of the beach?

63

Look for balance—Generally, a picture should not be split in half with equal areas on the top and bottom or on each side. Place a horizon line above or below the center of your photograph. Place figures off-center to make the composition more interesting. Try to balance large and small forms so they please your eye.

In Figure 36, the strongest horizontal line is above the center, and the figures are below center, so close to the bottom that this is an unusual composition. The rectangles of doorway, window, and signs are distributed nicely around the picture along with the brick pattern. There is a lot to see in this photo I made in a small English town; but your attention flows easily from one

Figure 36—How is the balance of this composition?

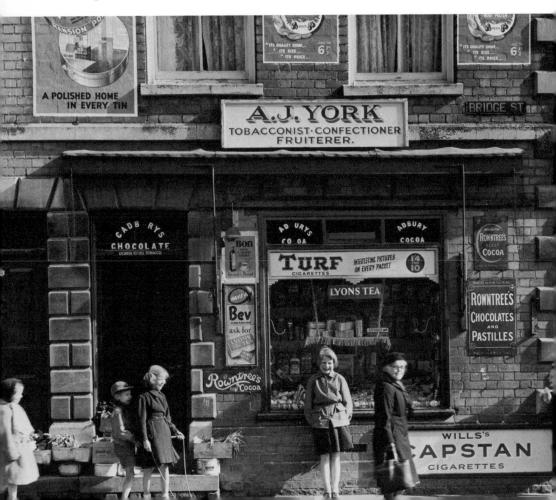

place to another. This harmonious flow is another guideline for good composition.

Look for contrasts—Place light forms or colors against dark forms or colors for contrast. Such contrasts help make an interesting composition.

Have a focal point—A pleasing composition has a main figure, group, form, or area, and less important figures or forms. The old barn in Figure 19 (page 36) is the main form there. Other parts of the picture seem to lead the eye to the barn. The lines of the fenceposts and the textures of hay and trees are less important but very necessary to the composition.

In a portrait the eyes are usually the most important features within the shape of a face. To prove this, check Figure 18 (page 35) and notice where you look first. Less important things will appear in the background of a portrait, which should be fairly simple.

Watch the background—Messy backgrounds probably ruin more pictures than any other photographic mistake. Be aware of telephone poles, wires, fences, jagged shapes, and blobs of color in the background of your slides or negatives. The background of Figure 37 is out of focus, a good way to keep a background in its place. The picture was taken in haste with a telephoto lens and could not be composed ideally. The three children and their expressions comprise the main element of the picture, but a plainer background would have been preferable.

Try framing—When you shoot through a dark area or through forms in the foreground, you frame your composition in an effective way. Maybe you have seen pictures of a baseball player

65

Figure 37—An out-of-focus background is one way of keeping a photograph simple.

sliding into base framed by the legs of another player. Figure 38 is an example of framing. The boys in the boat make a more interesting picture when seen through the black frame of a pier.

Use perspective and space—It is fun to photograph lines (such as a railroad track) or forms (such as buildings on a street) disappearing in the distance. Compositions that use perspective well can be dramatic.

Figure 39 with its feeling of space is another way of making the eye travel into the distance. I shot this with a 35 mm. lens on a 35 mm. camera at f/16, which allowed me to keep the whole picture in sharp focus from foreground to the far hills.

Painters like Cezanne showed us how to create a feeling of space with color. Cezanne often placed an area of color in the foreground of a picture and repeated the same color in the

66

Figure 38—This composition is improved because the boys are framed by the pier.

Figure 39—A feeling of space is often an interesting feature of a photograph. This is a scene in Colorado.

background near the top of the picture. The eye moves from one color spot to another, giving the feeling of space on a flat surface.

Look for mood—Though mood is not one of the elements of composition listed at the beginning of this chapter, it is important to think about. The expressions of peoples' faces sometimes set the mood of a picture. Lighting also creates a mood that may be happy, sad, or dramatic. In Figure 40 there is a

Figure 40—The way a picture is lighted contributes to the mood. My wife, Barbara Jacobs, shot this photo.

serious mood between conductor Zubin Mehta and actor Charlton Heston. They were photographed by my wife, Barbara, as they discussed a musical composition during a symphony rehearsal. She used a 105 mm. lens on a 35 mm. camera, which allowed her to stay far enough away not to disturb these men.

Symmetry—Many years ago composition was taught by rules of symmetry that are no longer used today. Symmetry is another word for balance. The way you balance lines, forms, color, and so on should be personal, when you have learned what pleases you and the people who look at your slides or prints.

Simplicity and other things—I have left the most important point about composition for last: keep your pictures simple. When the story you tell or the person you photograph is easy to see and the elements are well arranged, you have kept things simple within the photo. At first you must think about these things, but when you have taken enough pictures, you will compose carefully in the finder just as you ride a bike through a tight spot with ease.

There are a few other elements in a composition of which to be aware. These include patterns, odd shapes, and striking contrasts between large and small or fast and slow. Look at pictures you see in all kinds of magazines from *Life* to *Holiday* to *Look*. Try to figure out why certain pictures were chosen and how you like their composition. You will learn as much from the ones you don't like as from the ones you admire.

CROP YOUR PICTURES

To crop a picture means to cut off or mask along the edges. Often a print or slide can be improved when you hold a white piece of paper along one or more edges and ask, "Is this necessary?" Do this with small black and white or color prints before you have them enlarged. Show the printer where you want a print cropped by drawing lines on it with a grease pencil. Crop a slide by masking it with tape along the edges before you project it or have a print made. Removing unnecessary parts of a photo will often improve its composition, and tell your story with more punch.

Figure 41—Could this composition be more simple? Could the edges be cropped further? Is the background annoying? These are questions you must ask about your own prints and slides so you can improve them.

Since composition represents the way you see, learn to see clearly through the finder so your prints or slides do not have to be cropped. At first you should learn conventional balance. If you study or read about composition, you will become more secure with the camera. Then you can shoot pictures that are more unusual—and make them good! If you like a composition well enough to defend it, don't let what anyone says worry you, but listen to critics. You may discover how to improve a composition now, or when you shoot pictures again, in a way you did not see previously. Above all, keep your composition simple because then the important shapes, colors, or people will be clear to everyone and have the most impact.

5 | Is the Light Right?

How many different kinds of light do we see every day? Actually, just two kinds: daylight and artificial light from factory-made bulbs. Within these two categories, however, are many lighting effects that challenge camera fans. As you learn to use your camera, you also learn to recognize different kinds of light in order to take pictures at correct exposures.

DAYLIGHT

Bright sunlight—"Shoot with the sun coming over your shoulder" is an old saying that wise photographers *ignore* whenever they can. Though you are likely to shoot pictures in bright sun most often, its effect is more interesting when the sun slants from the sky at an angle on your scene or subject. You can even shoot into the sun with caution. When the sun is high

Figure 42—A killer whale leaps in bright sunlight coming from the left.

overhead near noon in summer, it is called top light. It creates dark shadows under the eyes, and it does not show the forms of mountains or buildings very well. At times we have to shoot in top light, but slanting sun at early morning or late afternoon is a lot more pictorial.

Notice how many photographs in *Holiday* or *National Geographic* are shot with the sun at an angle between sunrise and maybe 10 A.M. or from 4 P.M. until sunset. Landscapes are beautiful in slanting light, and its orange tint adds mood to a picture. In winter the sun never reaches high overhead in the United States, and all day its slanting rays are there for photographers.

Figure 42 was taken in midafternoon in spring with the sun at the left. The dark bulk of the killer whale contrasts against the background, the water sparkles, and the light shows forms well. The exposure with a 35 mm. camera was 1/500th of a second, which caught the animal in midair nicely.

Remember, your subject need not face directly into the sun and squint. People will be more comfortable with the sun at their sides or slightly behind them, and your pictures will be more interesting.

Hazy and reflected sunlight—A cloudy day or hazy sun may be very frustrating when you are photographing on a trip. We hope for bright sun to show forms and bring out colors in landscape pictures. However, if you cannot return, shoot in the light as you see it. Hazy sun produces pleasant pastel colors, and a Skylight filter adds warmth to color on a cloudy day.

Hazy sun is quite welcome for portraits. It is soft and easy on the eyes, and it doesn't create shadows that make a face look unpleasant. However, you need not wait for a hazy day

75

if you choose an outdoor shadowed area for your portrait "studio." If you can find a spot opposite or near a light-colored wall, you will have a natural reflector. Figure 43 is an example of what I mean. It was shot on my patio in the shade of my home. The girl's pretty face was lighted by sunshine reflected from a concrete patio and white wall. This soft, indirect illumination is the kind professional photographers spend thousands of dollars to achieve in a studio.

You may also make your own reflector to shoot portraits in shade. Apply crumpled aluminum foil to one side of a heavy piece of cardboard or ask about ready-made reflectors at the camera shop. You may also use a special white nylon umbrella, described later in this chapter. Any of these reflect light with few shadows. Your model is happy and your pictures glow.

Daylight indoors—Daylight coming through a window or glass door is also pleasant for portraits, though it may create too much contrast between the light and dark sides of a face. Figure 44 was taken by a window with a ready-made reflector on the left to brighten the shadowed side of the girl's face. An umbrella reflector would have done as well, or even a large white sheet of paper. If you want to shoot better-than-average portraits, experiment with reflected light. It can be beautiful.

Exposure in daylight—If you have a camera with a built-in exposure meter, you may wonder what there is to say about exposure in daylight. Generally, you can depend on your camera-with-meter, but there are ways to use it that insure more good pictures. First, read the instruction booklet that comes with the camera. It should tell you the basic ways of making a proper exposure. Then consider this list of things that can influence your getting good slides and prints:

76

Figure 43—Sunlight reflected from a light-colored wall is excellent for portraits.

1. Tilt the camera away from the sky, for too much sky will indicate a faster exposure than may be correct, and the result is dark slides or prints. However, if you are shooting a silhouette, expose for the sky.

2. Think about the brilliance of your subject. Bright white sand or snow sometimes give an exaggerated meter reading, and again your results will be too dark.

3. Be aware of backlighting, for it is the trickiest of all to expose for. Backlighting means you are shooting into the light,

Figure 44—Indoor daylight may be fine for portraits if there is enough light in the shadows.

Figure 45—Backlighting is tricky to expose, but its effects are often unusual.

and the meter indicates less exposure than your subject, who is in the shadow, needs. Figure 45 is an example of backlighting. Using a camera with a built-in meter, I moved close to the man for an exposure in the general shadowed area. Then I stepped back for an over-all reading. I set the f/stop between the two exposures for correct exposure of both sunlit and shaded areas.

When shooting in backlight, remember to open the aperture one or two stops beyond the exposure reading you get for bright sunlight. For instance, the sunlight reading for Figure 45 was f/11 at 125th of a second. The shadow exposure was f/5.6 at 1/125th of a second. I shot at f/8 at 1/125th between the two readings.

4. If you use a separate exposure meter, handle it the same way as you would a camera meter. If you can make incident light readings with your meter (measuring the light falling on a subject), you will find them useful against the light or in bright rooms that sometimes fool a reflected-light meter. Instructions with a separate meter will give you more details.

AVAILABLE LIGHT

When you shoot indoors without adding flash or floodlight, it is called "using available light." This type of light helps retain the character and feeling of a scene or subject, and may add mood to the picture. People are more comfortable in the natural light of a room and are less self-conscious about being photographed when flashcubes are not popping. In available light you need large lens apertures and/or slow shutter speeds, but depend on your meter for exposure time. Even if you need a tripod in available light, it may be more convenient than using flash and certainly your pictures will be more unusual. Of course, you need fast color or black and white films for best results indoors.

ARTIFICIAL LIGHT

Flashcubes and flashbulbs—There is no trick to using flash with simple cameras. You get best results between four and nine feet. If your 35 mm. camera uses flash, you can adjust the aperture for accurate exposure. On a carton or package of flashbulbs you will find a list of guide numbers for various types of film. Divide the number of feet from the camera to the subject into the guide number for your film. For instance, if the guide number is 80 and you are 8 feet from a subject, the answer is 10. That answer is also the f/stop at which you shoot, or f/10 (between f/8 and f/11 will do very well). Guide numbers are as simple as that, and the footage scale on your 35 mm. camera will tell you how many feet you are from somebody after you focus.

Joel Goss, aged thirteen, used a small flashbulb to photograph the action of a basketball game in Figure 46. The flash stopped action very well, but you will note that figures close to the camera are bright but those in the rear are darker. This is the way flash "falls off" when it is used at the camera. Only if Joel had used another flash unit off to the side would he have been able to light this scene more thoroughly. His picture was an award winner in the *Scholastic Magazine*/Eastman Kodak contest.

Electronic flash—When you find yourself taking enough flash pictures to wonder if the expense of cubes or bulbs is worthwhile, you might think about a small electronic flash unit. Electronic flash is used over and over, and all you need replace are the batteries. Electricity is stored inside the unit, and a flash tube gives off a bright, fast (1/1000th of a second) light when you snap a picture. Flash tubes are good for at least 10,000 flashes.

Many brands of small electronic flash units are available, starting at around 25 dollars. Their brand names include Honeywell, Braun, Spiratone, Ultrablitz, Vivitar, and Capro. The latest electronic flash units have a light-sensitive cell that determines how much light to throw according to your distance from the subject and its brightness. You don't need guide numbers with these new units that assure correct exposure, but they cost 85 dollars and up.

81

Figure 46—Joel Goss used one flashbulb to catch this tense moment of a basketball game.

In Figure 47 students in their school darkroom were lighted with one electronic flash unit held off to the right with a long cord attaching it to the camera. I moved the light away from the camera because it is more interesting and made the darkroom look more real.

Here is a checklist about electronic flash if you are wondering whether it is worth buying:

1. After you buy the unit, there are no additional expenses. Add up the annual cost of flashcubes or bulbs and decide whether the total almost equals a small electronic flash unit.

2. The very fast light is excellent for stopping fast action.

Figure 47—One electronic flash unit held off to the right created the feeling of this school darkroom.

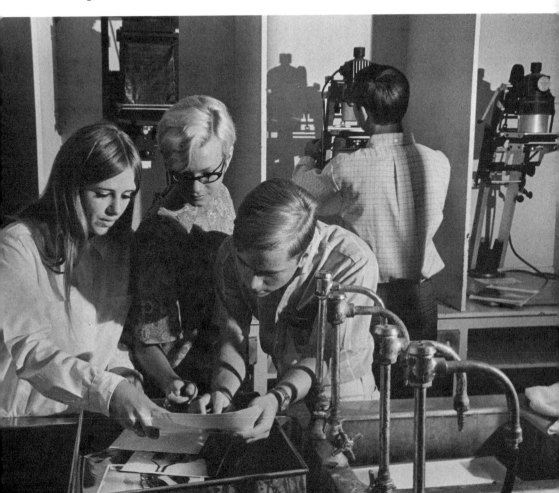

3. You carry one small unit rather than a lot of flashcube or bulb packages.

4. You can point the unit at a ceiling and "bounce" the light, which is more unusual and flattering than direct light from a unit on the camera. When you figure the exposure time for direct light by the guide number, open the aperture two stops for the average bounce exposure.

Electronic flash is not difficult to use, and can be very convenient when you think you are ready for it.

Using floodlights—The most advanced equipment you will use in lighting is floodlights. These are special lightbulbs, 250 or 500 watts, which are screwed into a reflector, or have their own reflector. The latter are called reflector-floods. When you feel ready to try this type of artificial light, here is a selection of equipment to begin with:

1. Two or three folding light stands

2. Two or three bulb sockets with 20 feet of wire attached to each; or two or three ready-made floodlight reflectors

3. Two or three Alligator clamps, which cost more than ordinary clamps but are much more sturdy

4. Two or three reflector-flood bulbs (for the sockets) or flood bulbs (for the reflectors)

This selection will cost between 35 and 50 dollars, but it will last a long time. You may have a case made to carry and store this equipment. Complete lighting kits are also available but cost more than a kit you assemble yourself.

When you use floodlights, you really learn how to make artificial light work in photography. Moving a light just a few

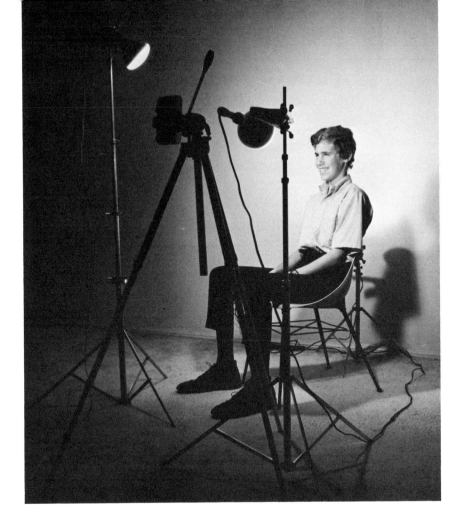

Figure 48—Typical floodlighting arrangement.

inches can change the appearance of a face or an object. The next four illustrations show how to use three lights for a simple portrait.

In Figure 48, the light at left (a reflector-flood) is the *main light* close to the front of the young man. The light at right is the *fill light* used to illuminate shadows caused by the main light. Behind the chair is a third bulb to light the wall. Figure 49 is the portrait I shot with the lights arranged as you see them in Figure 48.

85

Figure 49—Picture taken with lights set as shown in Figure 48.

In Figure 50, the main light is at the right and the fill light at the left is reflected into a white nylon umbrella made for photography. The portrait I made with this arrangement is Figure 51.

In both Figures 48 and 50 my 35 mm. camera is on a tripod.

The "studio" is my living room. By moving furniture and taking pictures off the wall, I have plenty of space for portraits. When I want a colored background, I hang a large sheet of colored paper on the wall.

There are many ways to light people and things with three floodlights. In color photography, photoflood bulbs are used with Type A Kodachrome and 3200°K bulbs with Type B Ektachrome. After you have learned to shoot with floods, you will feel like an "old master" of photography.

Daylight can be soft and beautiful, or harsh and awkward for your subjects. Look around for bright shadowed areas,

Figure 50—Floodlighting arrangement with umbrella reflector.

where people won't have to squint. Take advantage of early-morning or late-afternoon light, which make most outdoor scenes more interesting.

Floodlight shows you how a subject will look before you shoot. Flash on the camera is handy, but not usually very artistic. Electronic flash is worth the money if it will save you enough on flashcubes or bulbs. Bounced flash (when you can tilt a reflector at the ceiling) or electronic flash is much nicer

Figure 51—Portrait with lights arranged as seen in Figure 50.

Figure 52—Bounced electronic flash is a neat way to illuminate a group evenly without creating black shadows behind the people. These teen agers were getting their first look at a Polaroid print from an older-model Polaroid camera.

than direct flash. Figure 52 was taken with bounced flash, which does not leave black shadows behind people and covers a group more evenly than a flash at the camera.

Good lighting is a part of every worthwhile photograph, whether it is a slide or a print. The subject of lighting is complex and may require extensive study. You might also look at my book, *The ABC's Of Lighting* (AMPHOTO).

89

6 | Some Picture Ideas

Some photo fans carry cameras with them everywhere, and some think of pictures only when there is a party, a family gathering, a trip, or a school event. Which are you?

If you take a course in photography, the teacher gives assignments that are supposed to help you do new and different things with your camera. The picture ideas in this chapter are like assignments for you. Each idea is illustrated by a winning photograph taken by teen agers in the *Scholastic*/Eastman Kodak competition, except for one. These pictures were shot with 35 mm. cameras, and I hope they will inspire you to see the world around you a little better through your finder.

PORTRAITS

All pictures of people need not be taken with plain backgrounds. A few samples: outdoor portraits with foliage behind the subject

90

or pictures of people in the place they work. In any case, a candid, unposed portrait is often preferable to a studio-type picture, because a person can be more natural when he or she is unaware of the camera. Figure 53, entitled "Whistle While You Work," looks as though the girl was surprised by the photographer. It is an eye-catching shot by fourteen-year-old Marlene Larson.

Figure 53—A candid, informal portrait by Marlene Larson.

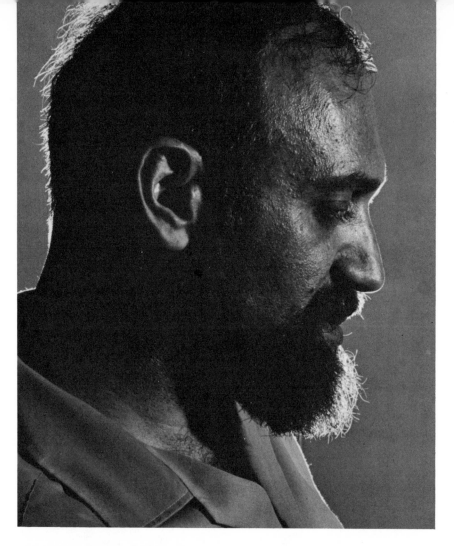

Figure 54—George Boldizar used backlighting very skillfully.

George Boldizar, seventeen, posed the man in Figure 54, but there is an informal feeling in the photo because the model is not looking at the camera. A strong light behind the head added an attractive outline. Notice how the top of the picture crops into the head, making the face more important.

I am not sure whether Bruce Aronson, seventeen, posed the dancer in Figure 55 or shot the action candidly. In either case,

92

Figure 55—This study by Bruce Aronson shows both character and intensity.

Figure 56—You sense more than how "Martha" looks in this portrait by Dennis Hart.

the portrait is dramatic and tells more about the model than how he looks.

Is "Martha" in Figure 56 self-conscious, or is this informal portrait a good composition of a modern young lady? Answer for yourself while I tell you that Dennis Hart, seventeen, placed his main floodlight slightly to the right of center and used a reflected fill light in the shadows. There was a normal 55 mm. lens on his 35 mm. camera.

Be a director when you shoot portraits by telling your models how you want them to turn or move but be ready for poses you don't expect. Animation and lively expression make portraits appealing.

SCENICS

Landscapes, seascapes, cityscapes, fields of flowers, sand dunes, and many details from nature are included in this category. While you are shooting, shift your camera slightly in each direction until the lines and forms pleasingly tell a story. Look for the dramatic as Tom Trindl did in Figure 57. He shot a horizontal picture first. In the darkroom he decided that a vertical section with clouds and three tiny figures made a better composition, and you see his imaginative cropping.

Bruce Cakebread, twelve, photographed Amethyst Lake in Canada, Figure 58, without a human figure, sometimes essential to a landscape. The shapes of land, the moody light, and the dark foreground give the picture impact. It is a design taken from nature, and beauty itself is the story.

Though Bob Noble is a professional photographer at Marineland of the Pacific, his picture, Figure 59, of sleeping sea elephants is one you could have shot—had you been lucky enough

95

Figure 57—Tom Trindl made a horizontal photograph and cropped a a vertical section from it in the darkroom.

96

Figure 58—This landscape by Bruce Cakebread is beautiful without the need of a conventional figure in it.

to visit the Mexican island of Guadalupe. He aimed a zoom lens into the Pacific sun and caught the sparkle of the water as well as the light glancing off the backs of the animals.

There are scenic pictures wherever you live or travel, but sometimes you must search for them. As an inspiration, you might look for books of Edward Weston's photographs in the library. (I'll list some titles at the end of Chapter 9.) Weston

Figure 59—Shooting into the sunlight dramatized Bob Noble's photo.

is one of my favorite photographers. He did wonders with ordinary trees, rocks, land forms, and water. Look carefully at
Edward Weston's compositions, for they are unusual and hard
to beat.

ACTION
Pretend you are a news photographer when you attend a sports
event or anywhere there is action. Try to snap your picture at

98

the precise moment when the ball is kicked or caught, or when a runner slides into base. This is called the *peak* of the action, and James Mandeville, eighteen, caught it as the surfer rode the crest of a breaking wave in Figure 60. Jim was perched at the end of a pier, aiming his 35 mm. camera with a 135 mm. lens. When you use long focal-length lenses, you bring action closer to your camera, but you can stay out of the way.

When you shoot action, you don't need to use your fastest shutter speed all the time. In Figure 61 Mark Packo, seventeen, used a slow shutter speed, about 1/15th of a second. He also panned, or moved, his camera in the direction of the runners as he snapped, which you recognize by the streaked background. The fascinating blur of legs and arms indicates fast action very effectively.

Figure 60—James Mandeville knew precisely when to snap this surfer.

Figure 61—Action photographed with a slow shutter speed gave Mark Packo an unusual effect.

NIGHT PICTURES

Taking pictures at night may be a mystery until you discover that a lens and film will record more dim light than you can see with your naked eyes. Slow shutter speeds or time exposures, fast film and large lens openings are all useful in the dark. You may have to guess the exposure time, unless you have a very sensitive exposure meter. Try several f/stops to get the correct one and, of course, use a tripod or something solid on which to rest your camera.

Figure 62 is another of Mark Packo's pictures. This night shot

100

of a small boat harbor helped win him a 1,000 dollar scholarship in the *Scholastic*/Eastman Kodak competition. Lights on the dock flared into bright star shapes, a pictorial effect that often occurs in darkness.

Francis Kittek, seventeen, shot a "Foggy Summer Evening," Figure 63, with a streetlight behind his models as they stood still for a two-second exposure. A sense of design is important at night because you are often working only with light and dark areas in the composition.

Shooting at night can be an adventure in city streets, in the snow, or anywhere that inspires you to take care and time for pictures. Your slides and prints will often make viewers ask how you did them.

Figure 62—Lights at night are attractive in Mark Packo's harbor scene.

Figure 63—A foggy scene may be difficult to capture excitingly, but Francis Kittek accomplished this shot with a two-second exposure.

102

Figure 64—Two floodlights enabled Gary Steelberg to picture his sister in a bubble bath.

FLOODLIGHTS

When you have floodlights to use, they can be very handy during the day or night. Gary Steelberg, fifteen, photographed his sister in a bubble bath, using two floodlights, in Figure 64. He directed one flood at her from above, and bounced the other against a white ceiling. With Tri-X Gary was able to shoot at 1/125th of a second at f/5.6.

As an experiment and for the fun of it, ask someone to model

103

Figure 65—Cindy Miller found a classroom to be an excellent setting for available-light pictures.

for you in a room where you can move about easily. Set your camera on a tripod, and use one floodlight only. Move the floodlight in a circle around your model at one- or two-foot intervals, and snap a portrait each time you set the light. The pictures will reveal more than words can do about the many effects of lighting.

AVAILABLE LIGHT

When there is enough light indoors to expose the film you are using, take advantage of the realism that available light creates. Simple cameras can rarely be used this way, but most 35 mm. cameras can.

A schoolroom is often bright enough for black and white photography, and Cindy Miller, seventeen, proves it with her candid shot, Figure 65, of a friend in class. Cindy exposed Tri-X at 1/60th of a second and f/4 when her friend was off her guard. Pictures without flash did not distract her model.

Bill Mielenz, sixteen, photographed a little boy by window light, Figure 66, which allowed him to shoot at 1/30th of a second at f/3.5. Had Bill taken the time to set up floodlights, he might have missed this story-telling expression.

Available light can be both rewarding and realistic. Many pictures you see in *Life* and *Look* were taken in available light with 35 mm. cameras.

FLASH AND ELECTRONIC FLASH

We know that a flashcube or bulb makes pictures possible with simple cameras anywhere. And we have seen how well electronic flash freezes action in Figure 47 (page 83). In Figure 67 Joel Goss may have used a flashbulb or electronic flash to shoot

105

Figure 66—Window light by itself dramatized this picture by Bill Mielenz.

these firemen at work near his home in Chattanooga. News photographers usually depend on flash to be sure they get the picture.

Make a few comparison shots of the same subject with flash and with available light. Decide which you prefer, and the next time you have a choice, you will be more aware of what your camera and film can do.

Figure 67—Joel Goss found flash to be very effective for this news photo.

Figure 68—Sharon Bailey maintained the realism of weak daylight in this playful scene.

108

DAYLIGHT

Daylight may seem easiest to use for pictures, but the picture ideas illustrated here are not the usual bright-sun variety. For instance, Sharon Bailey, seventeen, snapped two girls in Figure 68 after the sun had set. She was able to shoot at 1/60th of a second at f/5.6 with Plus-X to capture the spontaneous look of the girls playing. With a slow color film, such as Kodachrome II, she may not have been able to shoot this unless her lens opened to at least f/2.

Larry Lewis, eighteen, caught the last rays of the sun at the beach. He exposed for the bright water, allowing the two boys to become silhouettes, Figure 69. Larry didn't mind getting his

Figure 69—The setting sun provided Larry Lewis with just the right mood for this situation.

feet wet in the surf to shoot this lovely composition, and the boys hardly realized he was there. Much of the best photography you see in magazines and newspapers is done when people are least aware of the photographer at work.

The picture ideas in this chapter are only samples of the opportunities open to you when you are alert to picture situations everywhere. Photography is a hobby that can be very satisfying and can help make new friends for you. Don't just sit there! Take pictures!

7 | Making Movies

Keep in mind that movies are supposed to *move,* and you will be on the way to overcoming habits you may have learned with a still camera. This chapter only begins to tell you what movie-making is all about. You will know so much more after you have used a movie camera, discovered the skills you need, and experienced the thrills of movie photography.

MOVIE CAMERAS

When you look through the finder of a movie camera, you see through the lens the same image the film receives. When you press the shutter button, a motor pulls the film continuously behind the lens while a shutter called a gate opens and closes very rapidly (about 16 times a second). Image after image is recorded on the film, and when these pictures are projected

111

later at the same speed at which they were shot, the eye smoothly combines them so you see natural movement.

The most popular size movie camera is the Super 8, which uses 8 mm. film. Brand names include Kodak, Fujica, Vivitar, Sankyo, Minolta, Bauer, Canon, Nizo, Eumig, Konica, Nikon, and others. Most cameras are battery powered, and some have zoom lenses operated by hand or electrically. Almost all of today's movie cameras have automatic exposure systems that set lens openings to match the light. All you do is set a dial for the speed of your film.

Figure 70—Though this picture was taken with a 35 mm. still camera, it illustrates very well the guideline that movies should *move*. It is exciting to follow action with a movie camera; don't forget close-ups as well as more distant shots. Michael Charles, seventeen, shot this, and won a *Scholastic*/Kodak Award.

Figure 71—Five Kodak Instamatic movie cameras.

Movie-camera prices depend on the size of the lens, how the camera is powered, automatic features, and other things, such as the type of shutter and the range of the zoom lens. Simple movie cameras are not expensive, and more costly cameras are very easy to use. Figure 71 shows a selection of five Kodak Instamatic movie cameras. The least expensive at the left is $33.95, the one in the center is $68.50 and the one at the right, which includes an electrically powered zoom lens, is $103.50. Read the ads for movie cameras in photo magazines, send for brochures, and compare cameras before you talk to your dealer. When you buy, ask for a one-week or ten-day trial period. A simple camera without a lot of adjustments is best for beginners.

MOVIE FILMS

Kodachrome II, Ektachrome, Anscochrome, and Agfachrome are all made for motion picture cameras. The same film is used for both daylight and artificial light by placing a filter over the lens. Such filters are built into some movie cameras. Black and white films are also available.

113

MOVIE PROJECTORS

After your movie film is developed, you show it in a projector on a screen. Many brands of projectors are available at a wide range of prices. The newest ones include a system to drop in the film without having to run it by hand through the projector. Your father or mother can help you choose because projectors are too expensive to buy with your allowance. Advice from your local camera shop will be valuable when you choose a projector.

SHOOTING OUTDOORS

You think of still pictures one at a time as you shoot. However, each scene in a movie should be connected to the one before and the one after. If you have the time and inspiration, plan ahead. Make some notes about your movie story. Professionals call their plan for a movie a script. You can decide how you want your movie to begin, what action you want for various scenes, and how you plan to end the film.

On a trip or around home, you might begin with a wide-angle shot that shows where you are and who you are photographing. Figure 72 could open a movie with six teen agers at play in the surf. Next you might move closer to show two or three people splashing each other. Close-ups of faces can be intercut (set between other scenes) with more distant shots. Finally, you might zoom or move back to show the whole group sitting on the sand, tired and happy.

Movie composition follows the same guidelines as those discussed in Chapter 4. Try to arrange forms, figures, colors, and perspective so the eye sees a harmonious flow. In addition, you must be aware of how one sequence or camera angle will look in relation to others before or after. Change should not be so abrupt that the viewer is uncomfortable or loses track of your

Figure 72—A scene like this could open a movie.

story. Luckily, you can shoot scenes as you wish, and when you edit your film you can arrange the scenes in sequence.

Here are some hints for better movie-making:

1. Hold the camera steady; use a tripod when you want your pictures to look more professional. Pictures taken with a shaky camera make people nervous.

2. Turn, or pan, the camera smoothly from one side to another or up and down. If you pan too rapidly, the viewer gets dizzy when movies are projected.

115

3. Shoot more than a few seconds of film for a scene so your movie will not be jumpy. Four or five seconds might be a minimum at the beginning, and scenes that vary in length help make a movie more interesting.

4. Notice how much film is left in your camera before you start a scene. It is embarrassing to run out of film and miss good action.

5. Be sure your batteries are fresh enough to keep your camera operating. Take extra batteries with you on a trip.

Figure 73—At Marineland of the Pacific the dolphins jump quickly, dive into the water, and reappear for a reward of fish. The action takes five or six seconds. Be sure you have enough film left for such a scene when you are shooting.

6. Plan ahead when you can. Think of many ways to make your movies fun to see, such as: closeups, slow zoom shots, or surprising cuts from quiet action to more active situations.

7. Read a few books about making movies as you practice with your camera.

INDOOR MOVIES

Guidelines for outdoor movies apply to shooting indoors as well. The only difference is lighting. The easiest way to light indoor movies is to use a lighting bar made in various lengths into which you screw two, three, or four reflector-flood bulbs. Your movie camera is attached to the center of the bar, and as you turn the camera, the light follows. You may also use floodlights on a stand such as those shown in Chapter 5. As you experiment with taking movies indoors, you will find new lighting effects that achieve different moods.

EDITING MOVIES

To edit your movie film, you must cut the scenes apart and rearrange them in the order that best suits your story. You need an editing machine, which has two reels on it and a small viewer between them. You crank your film from one reel to the other, and watch the pictures in the viewer. When you see a section you want to cut out because it doesn't suit you, snip it and splice the remaining film together. Do this with a splicer, which cements two ends of film together with a chemical or with special tape.

Careful editing can eliminate out-of-focus or unpleasant movie footage and turn an ordinary reel of film into very interesting movies. Fit your sequences to show a beginning, a middle, and an end. You may also shoot special titles, made of cut-out letters

117

Figure 74—If this skier were part of your movie, you could place this action between two other scenes by editing. In this way you make sense of what you shoot and help eliminate footage you don't need.

or printed by hand, and insert them into your film. Most professional movies seen in theaters or on TV look smooth because a good editor has skillfully assembled the film to tell a story.

The art and craft of movie-making is fascinating when you shoot with a goal in mind. Take enough time to edit your film for the best effects. Just remember you are not making a series of action snapshots. A flowing story that holds the viewer's interest from beginning to "The End," will be more than just another "home movie."

8 | Pleasures of the Darkroom

Beginning photographers usually have their film developed and their prints made by a photofinisher. By the time you shoot four or five rolls of film in a month, it may be worthwhile to think about starting your own darkroom. You can save money, and even more important, you will enjoy the creative pleasure that comes with developing and printing your own pictures. Let's consider what you will need.

THE DARKROOM

You should not expect a fancy darkroom at first because you won't need it. Choose a bathroom, kitchen, part of a garage, basement, or attic. You need to cover the windows so no light comes through, and you need circulating air so you will be comfortable. You also need safelights in which to handle photographic paper. Check on them at your camera shop.

119

In my first basement darkroom I had a table for developing and enlarging equipment plus a small cabinet for supplies. You don't need running water in your darkroom. You can carry trays of water from a bathroom or laundry sink. Film and prints can be washed in the bathroom or kitchen.

You can make a work counter by fitting a piece of plywood across a bathroom sink. You might also darken the kitchen and use the sink counter there. If a room is dark enough at night, you may not need opaque shades on the windows. When you have an enlarger, you need more room, and a place to store it. My friend Harvey Hill built a rolling cabinet for his photo paper

Figure 75—The author's darkroom. At left are enlargers in two sizes: smaller negatives and 4 x 5 negatives. At right trays are arranged for developing prints. Paper and equipment are stored under the tables, and developing reels are hung at top right. Viewing light over hypo tray has a 40 watt bulb in it behind a diffuser. Darkroom is 5 feet wide and 12 feet long.

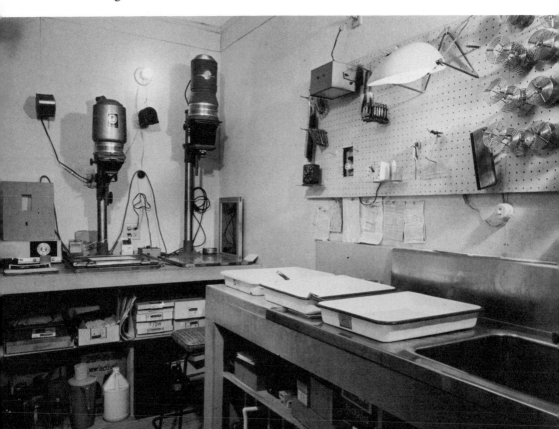

Figure 76—Harvey Hill's rolling cabinet is used in his kitchen at night.

and darkroom equipment, Figure 76. With his enlarger on top and his trays on the kitchen-sink counter, he does his darkroom work at night.

121

WHAT YOU NEED TO DEVELOP FILM

1. A developing tank; hard plastic is fine, but stainless steel won't break though it costs a lot more.

2. Developing reels. An adjustable plastic reel comes with the plastic tank. You can buy various sizes of stainless steel reels.

3. A darkroom thermometer; an inexpensive one will do very well.

4. A timer. Time and temperature are important for proper film development. You can use a watch or clock, or what is called an interval timer made for darkrooms.

5. Film developer. There are all kinds made by Kodak, Ansco, GAF, and other companies. Try one called Microdol-X or another called D-76, both made by Kodak. Or ask your photosupply store for a recommendation. If you want to increase the speed of black and white film, try Accufine. It boosts Tri-X to ASA 1,200.

Developers come in convenient cans or packages and are easy to mix. Store the developer in an airtight bottle. Add what is called replenisher after each roll to keep the developer a consistent strength. Follow instructions on developer and replenisher packages.

6. Film fixer, called hypo. Mix it from powder or buy it ready-mixed, and any brand will do. Hypo hardens the film and prevents it from being affected by light again.

7. A sponge or an old towel to keep your developing counter (and yourself) clean.

HOW TO DEVELOP FILM

The equipment and materials listed above are assembled in

Figure 77, plus a funnel to help when you pour into bottles or tanks. You also see the hands of my son Barry, eleven, holding an Instamatic film cartridge. He used his watch to time the development. Here are the steps to take:

1. Load the film in the reel in total darkness. Break the Instamatic cartridge carefully by striking it against a hard edge or lift the bottom cap of a 35 mm. cartridge with a bottle opener. Follow instructions with your tank or reel for proper loading technique.

2. Have your developer heated or cooled to 70°F. before you start. Fill the tank with developer. Place the loaded reel in the tank, and put on the top. Now you can turn on the light and check the time. Twist the reel in a plastic tank, or turn over a

Figure 77—Equipment and chemicals laid out for developing film. After the Instamatic cartridge is broken, the film is pushed into the reel at left. Developer is ready in the tank. When the film is in and the top is on, the reel will be turned with the small twirler.

stainless-steel tank a few times, every thirty seconds. This is called agitation, and it assures even development.

3. Develop for the length of time recommended by the film or developer manufacturer. The average is between six and twelve minutes. After you have developed a few rolls, you may want to add or subtract a minute or two, depending on the way your negatives look.

4. When the film is developed, pour the developer back in its bottle during the last fifteen seconds of the developing time. Run water into the tank through a light-tight hole in the top. Swish the water around and pour it out in about twenty seconds. Do not use acid with this wash water because it can cause tiny holes in your film.

5. Pour hypo into the tank, Figure 78, and agitate for ten or

Figure 78—When developer has been poured out of the tank and the film has been rinsed in running water, hypo is poured in. In ten or fifteen seconds the top can be removed and the film inspected.

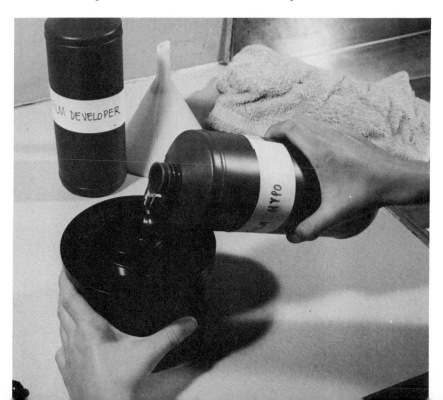

Figure 79—Film can be washed in the reel and tank. If you develop film very often, it is better to use a container with holes at the bottom, which allow water to run out.

fifteen seconds. Now you can look at the film if you are anxious. It will have a milky coating on it that dissolves in three or four minutes. Leave the film in the hypo for about ten minutes, and agitate it a few seconds each minute.

6. Pour out the hypo, rinse the film, and pour in a chemical called hypo neutralizer, such as Kodak's Hypo Clearing Agent. You use it over and over (up to twenty-five rolls per quart); this chemical reduces film washing time to only five minutes.

7. Wash the film while it is still in the reel by placing it under a faucet for five minutes, Figure 79. If you have a rustproof con-

125

tainer into which you can drill two or three holes along the bottom edge, this makes an even better film washer. I use a 5 x 5 stainless-steel tank to wash film.

8. After washing, soak the film in a chemical that helps it dry evenly, such as Kodak Photo-Flo. Hang the film from a clothespin on a line indoors. Wipe it carefully with a double sponge called a squeegee. You may also wipe it with a soft rubber car windshield wiper. The film will dry in one to two hours, depending on the humidity where you live and the temperature in the house.

HANDLING FILM AFTER IT IS DRY

1. Cut Instamatic-type film into two strips of six each, or strips of six if your roll is longer. Cut 35 mm. film into strips of six pictures, or frames, each. Store each roll in a separate envelope. Number and date it.

2. In a little notebook start an index of your film-roll numbers. After each number put a few words about what's on that roll. You may not shoot much now, but someday you'll be glad you can find old negatives easily.

3. Store your negatives in a box on a shelf or in a cabinet. Don't handle them any more than you have to, for negatives scratch easily.

PRINTING BLACK AND WHITE PICTURES

Contact printing means you lay a piece of photo paper on top of your negatives in a room, under safelights, and expose the paper to white light. The result is a contact sheet, or print, that shows each picture on the roll. You can study the frames with a magnifying glass, and decide which are worth having enlarged.

Here is what you need and how it works:

1. Use an 8 x 10 contact-printing frame. In Figure 80 Barry is using my 11 x 14 printing frame, and is ready to lay the photo paper atop the negatives. Negatives should be placed with the dull side up, and paper is inserted with shiny side down.

2. Clamp the back of the printing frame, turn it over, and expose according to the speed of the paper. You will learn this by a few experiments. Glossy paper is most suitable for contact prints.

3. You will need three 8 x 10 trays. Develop your contact print in the first tray in a paper developer such as Kodak Dektol. It should develop at least a minute, but if it takes two minutes, that's fine. If the prints look too dark after thirty seconds, make another print, because you won't get a correct series of tones in half a minute.

Figure 80—Film is laid with the dull side up and photo paper is placed on top of it with the shiny side down. Printing frame will be clamped closed and a contact print made. All this takes place in safelight, of course.

Figure 81—One of the pleasures of doing your own darkroom work is being able to use different developers. Mark Packo used Accufine on his Tri-X to get more film speed. This allowed him to shoot with a smaller aperture and get greater depth of field. This shot entitled "Varsity Team," helped win Mark his *Scholastic*/Kodak Award scholarship.

4. Dip the paper in the second tray for about ten seconds. This is a mixture of water and a small amount of acetic acid, and it is called shortstop because it stops development.

5. Move the paper to the third tray, which has hypo in it. This is the same chemical you use for film, but from a separate bottle. Film hypo will become too dirty if you use it for prints.

128

6. After prints have been in the hypo for about ten minutes, store them in another tray or in the sink until you are ready to wash them. Rinse the prints for a minute in running water, and soak them in Hypo Clearing Agent for a couple of minutes.

7. Wash the prints in a tray under running water for ten minutes. If you can afford to add another piece of equipment to your darkroom, print washers are made in different types and sizes. However, the least expensive gadget is a Kodak Tray Siphon.

8. Drain your prints and soak them in a flattening chemical such as GAF Flexigloss.

9. Dry prints on a flat surface. A metal shop will cut the corners round on a 20 x 30 piece of galvanized sheet iron, which is inexpensive. Check the prices of print dryers, for if you do much darkroom printing, you'll need one. If you use glossy paper, don't worry about drying it with the glossy side down on a ferro-type tin. A high-gloss surface is unnecessary, and it is far easier to dry this paper on a galvanized sheet, face up.

10. When prints are dry, put them under a weight for a little while so they won't curl.

ENLARGING BLACK AND WHITE PRINTS

The real fun of darkroom work is enlarging, because you can crop your pictures and make them big enough to see well. However, enlarging takes some skill, and I will cover the steps only briefly here. Check my book *How To Use Variable Contrast Papers,* listed at the end of Chapter 9. In it I cover enlarging very thoroughly for readers who want to know all the tricks.

1. Use the same trays and safelights mentioned for contact printing.

129

2. If someone in your family or a friend has an enlarger, find out how to use it. If you are buying an enlarger, an easel for the paper, and a timer for the enlarger and paper, advice from your photo-supply store will be very useful.

3. After placing a negative in the enlarger, move the lamp-head up or down to get the composition you want on the easel.

4. Enlarging papers are made in glossy and matte, or dull, finishes. A warm-toned matte paper is pleasant for portraits, while a colder-toned semigloss paper may be better for some

Figure 82—John Barringer, seventeen, was the first to see this very wide-angle photo because he developed his own film and made his own print. He also numbers his negative rolls and marks each enlargement with a roll and frame number so he can find the negative easily to make another. This was a *Scholastic*/Kodak Award winner.

scenic pictures you expect to hang. Most companies make sample books of their paper surfaces and tones. Investigate variable contrast papers, especially, because with a set of filters you need only one box of paper to get various grades of contrast.

5. Expose the print by first making a few test strips. Develop them as you did the contact print. Determine exposure time for the enlargement from the best test strip. Remember, a good print must have one or more deep blacks in it plus good, bright highlight whites. Between a deep black and a good white, a full scale of gray tones should fall naturally. You must experiment with grades of paper or variable contrast filters to match the right paper contrast to each negative. With a little experience this is not difficult, and the process is both creative and fun. Eventually, you will develop the ability to make and recognize a print that has beautiful, sparkling gradation.

6. Wash and dry prints as described before.

7. Enlargements sometimes have tiny spots of white or black on them from dust, scratches, or pinholes in the negative. You can get rid of these by diluting a special dye called Spotone #3 on a fine brush and darkening the spots.

8. Mount prints with dry mounting tissue and a hot iron or dry-mounting press, which someone may let you use. You may also use a spray adhesive such as Krylon #8010. Do not use rubber cement or glue because chemicals in these adhesives will stain your prints or make them fade.

COLOR DEVELOPING AND PRINTING

Until you shoot dozens of color rolls a month, it is not worth developing film yourself. However, making color prints is get-

131

Figure 83—Imagine the pleasure I had on first seeing this picture developing in the tray. This sunset in northern California is hanging in my living room, mounted on heavy cardboard with no border around it. A sheet of thin window glass covers the print, which is hung with plastic brackets.

132

ting easier, though it is trickier and more expensive than printing in black and white. Look at the Unicolor printing system which includes a drum developer. The basic kit is under 24 dollars, and the filter set is another 18 dollars. Other basic color-printing kits are also available.

TRICKY PICTURES

Once you have confidence with the everyday range of pictures you and your camera can shoot, you may want to try some tricky photos. Most of these require a darkroom or a very friendly laboratory that will spend time on your special pictures without charging too much. Here are four tricky pictures and how they were made.

Robert Bush, thirteen, skillfully combined three negatives to create Figure 84. The small center portrait of the girl was placed in contrast with the larger, dark profile. These two negatives were placed in the enlarger with a third negative of grass. The result is decorative enough to hang on the wall. Two or more slides can be mounted together in the same frame for double exposure prints in color.

Figure 85 was made from two negatives by Joan Fuller, fourteen. She painted opaque pigment in the center of the water negative, so it would be white when it was printed. She photographed the cat against a black background, and enlarged it along with the frame of water. The result is very unusual, and won Joan 100 dollars.

Paul Lierhaus, sixteen, photographed the man and railroad tracks on 35 mm. film. In his enlarger he projected the negative onto a piece of 4 x 5 Kodalith film that records only high-contrast black and white tones. He developed and dried the Kodalith positive image, and contact printed it onto another piece of

133

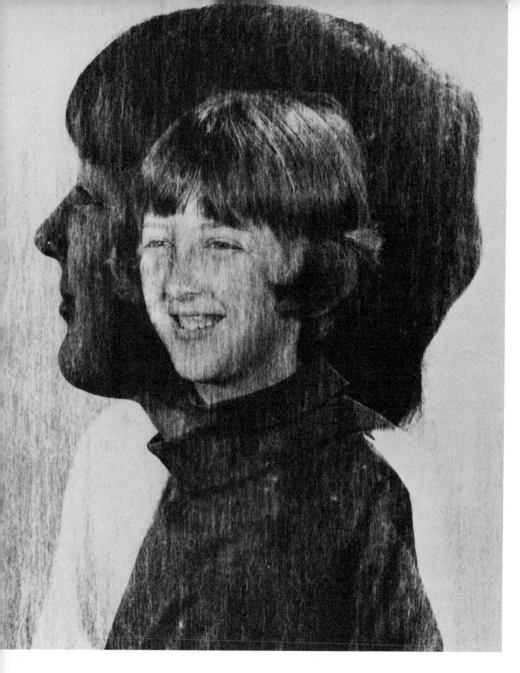

Figure 84—Three negatives were skillfully combined to achieve this effect.

Figure 85—Two negatives and some opaque paint yielded a highly original photograph.

134

Kodalith to get a negative. Then he made the print, Figure 86. This process is called "posterizing," and it can make an ordinary picture very exciting.

Figure 87 by Martha Gross, fourteen, isn't a photograph at all. It's called a photogram, and it was made by placing objects on a sheet of photographic paper and exposing the paper to light. Where the reel, scissors, and wire were placed, the paper was masked except for stray light under their edges. Martha also laid cut-out pieces of translucent plastic on the photo paper to give the background a pattern. Photograms can be very artistic when you use different objects such as sea shells, parts of a clock, or everyday objects. Move a few of the objects and expose the paper again to see the interesting overlapping shapes you get.

Now you have a good idea of what happens in the darkroom. Developing film is easy when you are careful to use the correct length of time and the correct temperature. Printing takes more skill and patience, but offers satisfying rewards. If you learn darkroom techniques, you should become a better photographer because you will make fewer mistakes when you take pictures.

Figure 86—Here the negative was projected onto a piece of film that records only high-contrast black and white tones.

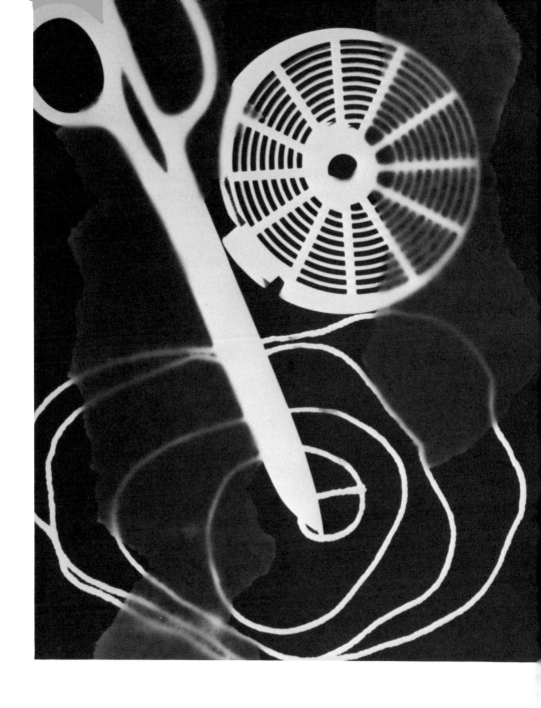

Figure 87—This is a photogram, made by placing objects on photographic paper and exposing it to light.

137

After all, you are the one who will have to correct those mistakes, and the more precisely your negatives are exposed and developed, the more quickly you can print them.

A famous photographer named Ansel Adams once said that we should see a picture in our mind's eye before we snap the shutter. Learning to work in the darkroom encourages you to do just that.

9 | Parting Thoughts

While writing this book, I have tried to cover the important guidelines and details that can help make photography a wonderful hobby for you. This last chapter includes an assortment of facts and ideas that were left over but are also important to the craft of photography.

TEN MOST COMMON PHOTOGRAPHIC FAULTS

1. Camera movement. Moving the camera probably messes up more good pictures than any other problem. Hold your breath at the instant you snap a picture. Squeeze the shutter. Don't jerk it.

2. Busy backgrounds. Be aware of everything behind and beside your main subject. Keep backgrounds as simple as possible.

139

Figure 88—Do any of the ten most common photographic mistakes appear in this picture? Possibly Number 2 with the cluttered background at left, but otherwise the composition is pleasing, the camera was steady, and the focus is sharp. When you get people involved in something, the result is a better family picture.

3. Prints and slides that are too light or too dark. With a simple camera, you cannot make adjustments for exposure. When you are ready to use a better camera, take exposure readings carefully. Some day all cameras will have automatic exposure systems that are almost foolproof.

4. Fog and light streaks on prints and slides. Load and unload your camera in the shade, not in bright sun that can get into tiny cracks in film cartridges.

5. Nervous movies. Handle the camera smoothly without panning too fast, jerking it up and down, or zooming too abruptly. Make a movie scene last four or five seconds at least. Otherwise viewers will just blink as your movies flicker by on the screen.

6. Empty compositions. In time you will know what a poor snapshot looks like. It has little or no story to tell. Somebody is standing in blank space, or there are meaningless objects cluttering part of the print or slide. A little imagination goes a long way to give composition more interest.

7. Faulty focus. When you shoot in a hurry, it may be difficult to focus accurately. You learn with practice to *see* sharp focus quickly.

8. Streaked Polaroid prints. You must pull the print from the camera in one consistent movement. Otherwise, the rollers will leave developing marks to mar the print. In cold weather, be sure to use the print warmer for good color.

9. The wrong exposure setting on your meter. It is easy to forget to reset the film speed on your camera's meter dial, or on a separate meter. Remember to reset it each time you change from one film to another, or your pictures will be too dark or too light.

10. Dirty prints or slides. Negatives and slides must be handled very carefully to keep them free of dust, scratches, and fingerprints. The care you take is worthwhile, especially when you have taken a lot of time and effort to shoot the pictures in the first place.

141

HINTS ABOUT PHOTOFINISHING

Camera shops, drug and department stores, and mail-order firms offer color and black and white photofinishing. This means they will develop your film and make slides or prints for you. The quality of this work varies widely. The least expensive may not be the best. My first choice would be a camera shop, because you will benefit by getting to know the people there. They send your film to a commercial photofinisher who needs a few days to a week to complete the work. Movie film is developed the same way.

You may also buy mailing envelopes for color film. The price of the envelope pays for the development. You simply mail your film to a laboratory and within a week slides or movies are returned to you. Some mail-order firms develop color-negative film and make prints for you. Payment is sent along with the film.

Your photo-supply shop will tell you the prices of color prints and how to order slides from your color negatives as well.

Black and white film processing and printing can also be arranged at your local camera shop. Have the film developed and a contact sheet made of each roll. Study the contact prints and choose those you wish enlarged. If you do not want the whole negative enlarged, mark the way you want it cropped with a grease pencil on the contact sheet. Prices and quality vary for black and white photofinishing. If you are not satisfied with the quality of your negatives or prints, if they are too light, too dark, dirty, or scratched, complain politely and ask that prints be made over. If careless work continues, find another photofinisher.

EDITING COLOR SLIDES

Not every slide you take is suitable to show friends or family.

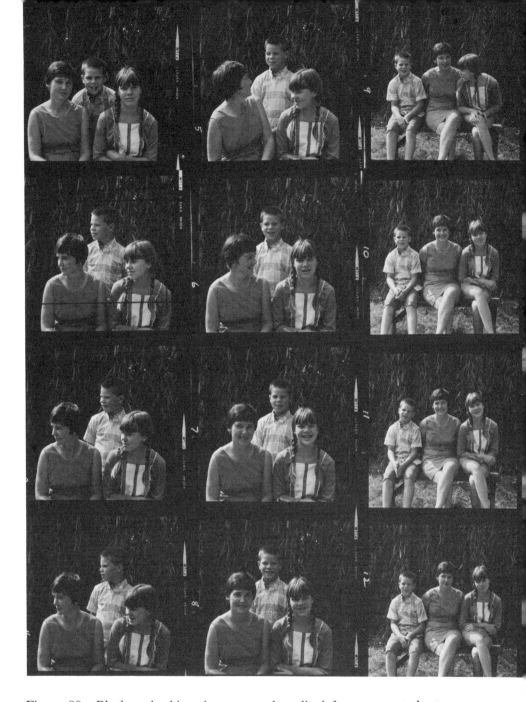

Figure 89—Black and white pictures can be edited from contact sheets like this one. Frame Number 2 (second from top on the left) has crop marks on it to show the printer how much to enlarge. These pictures were taken with a 2¼ x 2¼ camera so the contact prints would be easier to see in this book.

143

Figure 90—The quality of film developing and enlarging varies widely between photofinishers. This print of David Jaffee's, aged fourteen, *Scholastic*/Kodak Award winner has good blacks and nice tones, but it might have had too little or too much contrast if the photofinisher had not been careful.

Figure 91—You and your camera bring entertainment and pleasant
memories to anyone who sees your slides on a screen or looks at your
prints. When you become interested in photography, the whole world
looks a little more exciting in your viewfinder.

Pick out the slides that please you most and tell the stories you
saw in your camera finder. Put these in your projector tray and
store the rejected slides away neatly. By careful editing you will
not have to make excuses for fuzzy or pointless pictures. The
slides you *do* show will be more entertaining.

145

HOW ABOUT A CAMERA CLUB?

Joining a camera club at school or in your community can help you learn to make better pictures. You will be able to talk about photography with other interested people, and camera-club print competitions can inspire you to improve your camera work. Try not to get bogged down in talk about equipment and gadgets. Discuss composition and camera technique in order to get the most from camera club membership.

Figure 92—George Berke, sixteen, entered this picture story on the Brooklyn Bridge in the *Scholastic*/Kodak Award contest—and won an award. The way George shot different moods and angles of the bridge is a good example for both still- and movie-camera users. When you can explore a subject from many points of view, you get more interesting photographs.

CONTESTS

Some photographic contests are worthwhile if the prizes are appealing and if the sponsor does not keep your prize-winning pictures. If you must give up your slide or negative in order to win a prize, think twice about entering a contest. It feels good to win and prizes may be rewarding, but you must balance this against losing your photograph. The contests held yearly by the *Saturday Review* and by *Scholastic Magazine* with Eastman Kodak are two of the best.

PHOTOGRAPHIC SCHOOLS AND COURSES

Many high schools offer courses in photography, and if you are interested by all means take such courses. Instruction and equipment available to you will be a head start towards improving your skills. Someday you may want to study photography in a college or specialized school. This is a good way to learn thoroughly if you intend to make a career of working with a camera.

FLUORESCENT LIGHT AND COLOR

If you have ever taken a color picture by fluorescent light, you know how faces and flesh tones turn green. Something in a fluorecent tube does this, and you need a correction filter to avoid the greenish look. For a list of the right filters, check Kodak Data Book E-76 entitled *Applied Color Photography Indoors*. Several companies make correction filters if you must shoot color under fluorescent light.

ALMOST THE END

In many ways today's cameras, films, and photographic services seem to make photography too easy. I'll explain this, but first let me tell you about the early days of snapshot pictures, when

147

Figure 93—Scenic pictures are very popular among all photographers, and this one by Dennis Bresnahan, seventeen, is excellent because Dennis studied photography in high school. This is also a *Scholastic*/Kodak Award winner.

your grandfather or greatgrandfather may have had his first box camera. In 1888 a man named George Eastman invented photographic film on rolls. (Before that negatives were made on individual sheets of film.) Eastman sold a box camera with a roll of one hundred negatives in it. After all the pictures were taken, the whole camera was sent to the factory, the film developed, prints made, and the loaded camera returned to the owner. Mr. Eastman made up the word "Kodak" for his camera, because the word had a good sound to it. He also used this slogan in his advertising: "You push the button, we do the rest."

That slogan is even more true today. Cameras include all sorts of automatic features to make picture-taking easier. But it is still the person using the camera that is in control. Only *people* have eyes to see composition and color, and only people like you can decide when to take a picture. Please enjoy today's easy-going cameras and equipment, but when you push the button, keep in mind that the more you know about the craft of photography, the better your camera and you will "do the rest."

I hope you get a lot of wonderful pictures. I wish I could see all of them.

Glossary

Aperture—The opening of a lens; its size is adjusted by the diaphragm.

ASA film speed—A number by which the sensitivity of a film is measured; the higher the number, the faster the film.

Backlighting—Light that shines on a subject from the direction opposite the camera, or towards the lens.

Contact print—A print made by placing negatives tightly against photographic paper and exposing the paper to light. A contact print of a roll of negatives is a *proof sheet*.

Crop—To trim or mask a print or slide along one or more edges to improve composition.

Cut—In movie making, to switch from one scene or view to another.

Darkroom—A light-tight room or area where film may be developed and photographic prints made.

Depth of field—The distance range between the nearest and

farthest objects that appear in focus in a photograph. Depth of field depends on the lens opening, the focal length of the lens and the distance from the lens to the object.

Diaphragm—A circle of overlapping metal leaves that open and close within a lens to control the amount of light that reaches the film.

Easel—A device used to hold photographic paper flat while making an enlargement.

Electronic flash—A light source powered by batteries or house current. The flash is very fast and can be used about 10,000 times before replacement.

Emulsion—A thin coating of light-sensitive material in which the image is formed on film and photographic papers.

Enlarger—A kind of vertical projector used to enlarge a negative on photographic paper.

Floodlight—A light source for photographs, either in a separate reflector or a bulb made with its own reflector.

Focus—To adjust the distance setting on a lens so the subject is sharp on the film.

f-stop—A term used to indicate the aperture or lens opening; the f-stop number is used to determine proper exposure.

Grain—Tiny texture that may appear in a negative, print, or slide; grain results from the specks of silver in the film emulsion, and is more noticeable in fast films than in slow ones.

Highlight—The brightest area of a subject, or as it appears in a negative, print, or slide.

Hypo—A chemical used to fix film and paper so it will not be affected by light.

Lens focal length—The distance from the lens to the film, usually measured in millimeters; longer focal length gives a larger image, and shorter focal length gives a wider angle image from a given point.

Normal lens—The lens that usually comes with a 35 mm.

151

camera, and which photographs a scene nearly as the eye sees it. A normal lens has a narrower view than a wide-angle lens and a wider view than a long focal-length lens.

Pan—To move the camera from one side to another or up and down to follow the action of a subject.

Photofinishing—The commercial development of film and production of prints and slides.

Rangefinder—A device used on a camera that uses two overlapping images as an aid to focusing.

Reel—The part of a film-developing tank into which film is wound and held while being processed.

Safelight—A special light for the darkroom under which photographic paper may be handled safely.

Shortstop—A small amount of acetic acid in water, used to stop development in a print, and to make hypo last longer.

Single-lens reflex—A camera in which the image is viewed through the lens and reflected by a mirror into the finder where the image can be composed and focused.

Simple camera—An inexpensive camera on which lens openings cannot be adjusted and which cannot be focused.

Slide—A color picture, also called a transparency, which is mounted for projection on a screen.

Spotting—The elimination of small dust spots or scratches on a photographic print by means of a diluted dye and a fine brush.

Still camera—A light-tight box with a lens on one side and film inside which takes pictures one at a time.

Tank—A container for chemicals in which film is developed or washed.

Telephoto lens—A lens that makes a subject appear larger on film than does a normal lens; a telephoto brings a subject closer like a telescope.

Transparency—A color slide.

Wide-angle lens—A lens that has a shorter focal length and a wider view than a normal lens.

Zoom lens—A lens in which the focal length can be adjusted over a wide range, giving the photographer, in effect, lenses of many focal lengths.

153

Further
Reading

There are many fine books about photography, as well as books of photographs that have lasting value. When working with a camera becomes a more serious hobby, you will want to read some of these books and begin building your own library. You should read what other writers have to say about cameras, darkroom work, and all the techniques of this fascinating craft. You should also be familiar with the best that has been done by fine photographers over the years. The list of books below is only a beginning. Some were not written for young readers, but I think you will find them useful anyway.

Look for these books at your local library or camera shop, or write to the publisher, AMPHOTO, 915 Broadway, New York, N.Y. 10010, and ask for the latest catalogue. AMPHOTO publishes only books about photography.

Bennett, Edna, *Tabletop and Still Life Photography*. New York: AMPHOTO, 1970. How to shoot small objects and make compositions on a tabletop.

Caulfield, Patricia, *Complete Guide to Kodachrome II and Kodachrome X*.

154

New York: AMPHOTO, 1964. A fact-filled introduction to these two very popular films by a former photographic-magazine editor.

Foldes, Joseph, *Everybody's Photo Course*. New York: AMPHOTO, 1966. How, when, and why of making better pictures is shown photographically.

Gaunt, Leonard, *How to Choose and Use Your 35 mm. Camera*. New York: AMPHOTO, 1969. A guidebook for selecting a 35 mm. camera and other equipment.

Jacobs, Lou, Jr., The ABC's of Lighting. New York: AMPHOTO, 1962. This is a handbook on lighting. Included are discussions of daylight, available light, floodlight, and flash.

————, *Electronic Flash*. New York: AMPHOTO, 1971. All about electronic flash, for the beginner as well as the serious photographer.

————, *How to Use Variable Contrast Papers*. New York: AMPHOTO, 1970. A detailed discussion of darkroom work.

Keppler, Herbert, *How to Make Better Pictures in Your Home*. New York: AMPHOTO, 1962. Hints on photographing your family and friends at home.

Kinzer, H. M., *Available Light Photography*. New York: AMPHOTO, 1964. How to shoot in poor lighting conditions and get good pictures.

Matzkin, Myron, *Better Super-8 Movie Making*. New York: AMPHOTO, 1967. A good book for the beginner who wants to make professional-type movies.

Mannheim, L. A., *Do Your Own Film Processing*. New York: AMPHOTO, 1969. All the details for developing your own film.

Petzold, Paul, *All-in-One Movie Book*. New York: AMPHOTO, 1969. A basic book about movie photography for the beginner.

Rothstein, Arthur, *Color Photography Now*. New York: AMPHOTO, 1970. A brief history of color photography, plus a lot of information about what happens when you shoot color. Mr. Rothstein is chief photographer at *Look Magazine*.

Szasz, Suzanne, *How I photograph Children*. New York: AMPHOTO, 1971. A guide to taking pictures of children by a woman who is well known for her photography.

Tydings, Kenneth S., *Self-Teaching All-Camera Photography*. New York: AMPHOTO, 1963. How to use many different kinds of cameras and make better pictures.

Wallace, Carlton, *Making Movies*. New York: AMPHOTO, 1965. A good introduction to the art and craft of movie-making including hints for being more creative.

Weisbord, Marvin, *Basic Photography*. New York: AMPHOTO, 1966.

155

Step-by-step explanation of photography for the beginning snap-shooter.

Wersen, Kathy, *ABC's of 35 mm. Photography*. New York: AMPHOTO, 1964. How to see creatively, how to use lenses, choose lenses, choose films, and use the darkroom.

Wright, George and Cora, *Guide to Perfect Exposure*. New York: AM-PHOTO, 1967. All about exposure indoors and outdoors, color and black and white, with and without exposure meters.

Woolley, A. E., *Traveling With Your Camera*. New York: AMPHOTO, 1965. Hints for getting the best pictures when you travel.

A Few Favorite Books of Photographs

Cartier-Bresson, Henri, *The Decisive Moment*. New York: Simon and Schuster, 1952. A famous French photographer who is a master of candid, available light pictures, discusses photography.

Photography Annual. New York: *Popular Photography*. Each year a new Annual presents pictures and techniques that may inspire you when you use your camera.

Pollack, Peter, *The Picture History of Photography*. New York: Harry N. Abrams, 1958. One of the best histories of photography with a fantastic collection of old photographs, shot before any of us was born.

Weston, Edward, *California and the West*. New York: Duell, Sloan and Pearce, 1940. This is more than thirty years old but worth finding in the library to study Weston's compositions.

Index

1 2 3 4 5 75 74 73 72 71